T0065515

# TRUMP BECOMING MACBETH

WILL OUR DEMOCRACY SURVIVE?

DONALD A. COLLINS

authorHOUSE®

*AuthorHouse™*
*1663 Liberty Drive*
*Bloomington, IN 47403*
*www.authorhouse.com*
*Phone: 833-262-8899*



*Published by AuthorHouse 06/17/2021*

*ISBN: 978-1-6655-2912-9 (sc)*
*ISBN: 978-1-6655-2911-2 (e)*

*Library of Congress Control Number: 2021911944*

*Print information available on the last page.*



*This book is printed on acid-free paper.*

# DEDICATION

Dedicated to Sarah G. Epstein with whom I've shared a blissful journey for 27 years.

# CONTENTS

# INTRODUCTION

By the time these Op Eds are read much will have changed. In fact. Trump may even be indicted for his behavior by some entity. But the arrogance that attended his Presidential term in office and his behavior afterward has had enormous effect on American politics which will malinger in our history forever. His role and influence in the January 6, 2021, U.S. Capitol insurrection will be marked in perpetual ignominy.

So why another book about facts which are now so well proven? Simply to raise the level of understanding of my op ed readers and other possible audiences and state an urgency for repair before time passes and all is lost.

Also, to acknowledge that the text, sans the substantial electronic options which were added, allows me to offer my heartfelt thanks for years of support to my editors Declan and Lola Heavey, whose powerful web site located in London attracts support from Nobelists and many other credible experts on a variety of cogent topics. Go to www.churchandstate.org.uk to access my material under "Authors" and find its other visionary materials.

With those caveats let me begin. What you will get, as my texts are, with some editing, the text parts of my op eds which have been written mostly within the past year, sans the electronic add on options.

Should any of my books be sold, all proceeds will be donated a US NGO, International Services Assistance Fund, which I founded in 1976 and which has since worked tirelessly for programs which offer women family planning options.

To repeat, I have taken a number of my Church and State op eds and with the London editors permission edited them as the main text for this book.

Donald A. Collins
Washington DC.
June 13, 2021

# CHAPTER 1 WHEN WILL TRUMP REALIZE HE'S MACBETH? NEVER, BUT AMERICANS WILL!

*3 June 2021*

Remember the famous Shakespeare play Macbeth in which the returning hero of war murders the king in order to become king and sets forth a series of events that lead him finally to understand what his humongous behavior has bought him when, at the suicide of his only truly close ally, his wife, he says: "Life's but a walking shadow, a poor player, / That struts and frets his hour upon the stage, / And then is heard no more. It is a tale / Told by an idiot, full of sound and fury, / Signifying nothing."

Donald J. Trump I imagine will likely never get there. He will never apologize. But in trying to murder our fragile democracy using hate, lying and his inherited wealth to take whatever route to power he could use, this disgraced former president is now faced as Macbeth was with an army of outraged citizens of both parties who are coming to displace him forever from political power and quite possibly put him in jail. Does he even have as Macbeth did any close ally?

Those elected officials who cluster about him in his coming precipitous fall must surely know their racist driven, power seeking fealty can't survive the morality test to which the majority of Americans will hold them!

Our democracy, despite the darkness of the political present, will survive and as we overcome the racism of 400 years of slavery, America will continue to show the world the vast benefits of our system of law and order even as we understand the heinous flaw of slavery which has always infected many world human populations since their inception!

We in time surprisingly may look back and thank Trump for exposing the worst in us so we could move on to fulfill the best in ourselves!

# CHAPTER 2 TRUMP AND HIS GOP LEADERS ARE DESTROYING OUR DEMOCRACY!

*1 June 2021*

All elected politicians need now to react powerfully to the GOP attempt to steal our democracy represented by Republican Senate Minority Leader Mitch McConnell's personal request to his senate colleagues to vote against a January 6th Commission!

This Trump instigated act is so dangerous that the real response must be the massive rejection of any anti-democratic elected official, which basically means the 35 Republican Senators who went along with the evil McConnell choice; just as many Republican-led state leaders are bent on passing laws that reduce votes from qualified minority voters while claiming voter fraud is a danger, when it is not!

This echo of the effect of Trump's claim of the big lie about the November 3, 2020, Presidential election, is critical in our understanding why our fragile democracy is in deep trouble!

Hence my urgent advice is that the majority of our important corporations better now step up and see that these aberrant politicians get the message that the GOP can't steal our democracy.

One way would be not giving money to those people.

Another would be for our major media providers to ensure that these dangerous GOP lies get exposed at every opportunity!

We already know that many members of the GOP are repelled by the behavior of its top leaders, but apparently too many fail or refuse to understand that the winning of the next election at the cost of destroying democracy is not related to an election choice but to a turn to tyranny!

American democracy is at a crossroads, but we can hope that our corporate leaders can realize their continuing business self-interest means this unacceptable GOP behavior must be interdicted ASAP.

# CHAPTER 3 GOP LYING MAY NOT BE AS BAD AS ITS INCOMPETENCE!

*31 May 2021*

The Princeton report on ways to substitute non fossil fuel energy capacity by 2050 encourages one to see real possible progress toward fixing our earth's climate.

Read these articles here and here.

The GOP's current unwillingness to fix adequately our aging infrastructure illuminates their gross incompetence to see the best way for America's future.

Thus, my main point: the GOP's blatant lying for short term political gain for Donald Trump may not be its most dangerous fault, but failing to face major challenges to achieve long term gains such as to avoid climate disasters IS!

And after 47 years of Roe working well, we now find the potential for further GOP incompetence as the Supreme Court takes up the Mississippi abortion case which would reduce choice at a time when the need to rein in population growth looms as another crisis requiring competence not mindless GOP ideology.

Lots of Republicans get my point and even Catholic Joe Biden gets it right on choice.

It's not about politics or ideology, it's about human survival. The surfeit of human numbers, now having grown from 2 billion to almost 8 in my 90 year lifetime on our planet, needs us to offer every safe method for reproductive choice.

And sorely needed is full understanding of the urgency for pursuing global needs such as providing vaccines to India, Brazil and all who need them, not thinking that we can delay giving all humans on earth as rapid access as possible.

In short, global actions based on science offer the only sustainable path to a peaceful future. Yes, the USA could offer the world a workable example, but the gross incompetence of one of its two political parties makes it harder if not impossible!

The incompetence danger is further enhanced by Senate Minority Leader Mitch McConnell's demand that his Republican colleagues do him a "personal favor" and vote against a January 6th commission investigation. A lot of honorable Republicans found this abhorrent including Alaska Senator Lisa Murkowski whose outrage you can read about here.

Hard to decide which is worse, the lying or the incompetence, but together they make a lethal attack on progress on vital issues long settled by science and moral probity.

# CHAPTER 4 OVERPOPULATION: LIMITS GET TESTED AND FAIL!

*29 May 2021*

As what in my recent OpEds I have dubbed the "Attenborough crisis"—too many human consumers of Earth's limited resources—we get daily examples such as the page one May 27 Wall Street Journal story entitled "A Grand Plan To Vaccinate The World Unravels" which you can read here.

The climate crisis has caused a growing demand that Exxon, Shell and other fossil fuel producers reduce emissions ASAP!

In a recent TV interview, the 95 year old master scholar of our natural world's limits, Sir David Attenborough, predicted another 3 billion human consumers will be added if current growth rates prevail. We now have 8 billion human consumers, up from 2 billion in his lifetime.

It is obvious that reductions of all over consumption is now required but far from certain to occur!

It now appears that most likely saviors of humans peacefully continuing to live on Earth over the long term will have to be big corporations, the most enlightened of whom will fear the loss of their hegemony.

Can enough vaccines be provided for all in this world? Not now on a timely enough basis, but as soon as corporations see the clear self interest in so doing, just as fears about dangerous climate resolutions are now hitting Exxon and Shell.

In short, could profits and fear combine to let corporations save sustainable life on Earth? Let's see.

# CHAPTER 5 TRUMP ON TRIAL, DEFINITELY, BUT LIKELY MONTHS FROM NOW!

*28 May 2021*

Recall that the notorious 1930's Chicago mobster Al Capone, was never convicted of being behind multiple murders, only income tax evasion. He was convicted in 1931, the year I was born in Evanston, a Chicago suburb, where my father worked as a bond salesman at the time. You can read Capone's Wikipedia bio here.

Will Trump likely pay for his murderous crime of inciting the January 6th insurrection on the U.S. Capitol or even perhaps for his numerous questionable actions while in office? We will probably not know for months but the NY District Attorney's empaneling of a grand jury suggests his past business practices may prove extremely actionable. Expect news before Manhattan District Attorney Cyrus Vance Jr's retirement at year end 2021.

We can count that the full trial process will likely take months as everyone is lawyered up to the hilt. You can read an initial Washington Post story here.

The growing number of alleged stories of wrongdoing by former U.S. President Donald J. Trump and his minions should at least serve to warn the GOP that his political power may well not survive the midterm elections if then.

Michael Cohen, his longtime attorney, wrote a book entitled "Disloyal" whose validity could be contested in any trial for obvious reasons of self-interest, but Thrift books analysis is interesting reading here.

Perhaps the most telling of recent disclosures was the brief May 26 CNN interview with former wife of the son of Trump's long time CFO, Jennifer Weisselberg which is partly covered here.

Facts of what Trump has perpetrated against our democracy just don't get any more disgraceful and the comparison with the fate of Al Capone makes the life story of that heinous murderer seem almost worthy of pity. After years in prison, Capone was paroled to his home and died with dementia and pneumonia at 48.

# CHAPTER 6 HAVE GOP LEADERS LIED THEIR PARTY TO EXTINCTION?

*26 May 2021*

The list of "slanderous myths" lengthens daily—as Michael Gerson's May 25th OpEd tells us, which you can read here—but like any dead body as it decays, it still attracts attention and adherence from such weird souls as QAnon believers and other far right voices, aided and abetted by Trump and the other big elected GOP leaders and endorsed by Fox, a source exiled as untrustworthy by every credible news source!

Is it time for a new political party, just as it was in 1856 when the GOP ran its first candidate?

Perhaps we could think up the new party's name and its proposed principles, perhaps citing those principles first!

Former or current disaffected GOP leaders could meet to give voters a list of the new party's principles.

Here's where the likely impracticality of a new party surfaces.

For example, a majority of Americans cheered Liz Chaney for calling out Trump on his big lie, but few Democrats and independents would agree with her views on choice or other cultural positions.

Mitt Romney, a Utah Mormon, has other similarly non-winning biases.

John McCain is dead, and no liberal Republican Governor seems ready to take up the task for building a new franchise.

So here we are, moderates with only one party we can support, a party which perhaps is being pushed too far leftward.

However, looks like by 2022 we will be seeing big spending not fully embraced by all Democratic voters but still repelled by the GOP.

So, I am guessing that Democrats are going to do the exception and win in an off-year election.

If Trump is indicted before November 2022, Democrats surely keep Congress even if only with a slim majority. Sadly, even though the lies have not killed the GOP, the GOP does not qualify as a credible co-equal partner in our needed two-party democracy, a democracy, thanks to Donald Trump, which remains under constant assault by crazy voices including his.

# CHAPTER 7 IS THIS THE BEGINNING OF THE END OF A FUNCTIONING DEMOCRACY?

*22 May 2021*

No January 6th Commission investigation apparently, says Republican Leaders of both Houses Mitch McConnell and Kevin McCarthy, no agreed upon legislation for needed infrastructure, no admission from the Dictator in Chief Trump that he lost on November 3rd — in short the kind of continuing big lies that brought Adolph Hitler to power in the 1930's!

But this is prosperous; democratic USA being hornswoggled by the party of Lincoln.

Biden is keeping cool, and the swelling disbelief and outrage keeps growing as progress with COVID-19 here in the USA seems on track, but certainly not elsewhere — in India and Brazil for examples.

But everyone is coming to realize that we are part of a world growing more dysfunctional daily.

And the variant strains of the COVID are multiplying in many countries while vaccines there are scarce and many governments shaky.

Our thesis is being daily confirmed that 8 billion human consumers exceeds our earth's capacity to sustain us peacefully.

So instead of facing this urgent threat, the world's greatest democracy is avoiding positive governance and admitting the overpopulation problem exists.

Biden at his age and as a likely one term President is not likely to step forward, tell the truth and initiate important actions to make women's reproductive rights more available, steps which history would subsequently view as a master stoke but probably won't help his party win in 2022!

Dismissing what many members of both the GOP and the Democratic Party advocate, the vital need for a strong 2 party system has broken down seemingly beyond repair.

What to do? Is this the beginning of the end of a functioning democracy?

Could be.

# CHAPTER 8 GROWTH IS A CANCER WITH APPARENTLY FATAL PLANETARY APPEAL

*17 March 2021*

What I have written here was inspired by a letter received from knowledgeable friends who had pondered this question of why so few of us seem worried about population growth. Their email to me can be found below.

Many distinguished scholars have written often on this site and elsewhere about the growth of human numbers.

For example, in my 90 year old lifetime population has gone from 2 billion to nearly 8 billion today. In short, there has been a cancerous like growth problem of human numbers which we must solve or face diminution in the quality of life on earth.

Optimists argue that things are getting better all the time, fewer are starving, etc. and that our population growth is healthy and sustainable. Forever??

Despite presenting the scientific validity against such Pollyanna projections by many eminent experts such as Sir David Attenborough no real effort from top world leadership speaks to the urgency of at least trying to stabilize numbers now and then seeking to reduce our human numbers over time.

The “why not” to that position is that growth is being constantly flogged by most of those in power and by mindless behavior about human reproduction by the majority of us humans.

Huge pushers for growth are the world’s religions which seek to match numbers against each other worldwide. Even as the numbers of believers has declined in many places including the USA, the atheists or other nonbelievers are loath to attract attacks from these oft violent believers. So even though the unchurched or non-mosque goers must not be unhappy to find more and more people are not being religious, but they don’t provide many voices against population growth.

The kind of insanity pushed by religion is exemplified in the attachments below.

Then large nations such as China or the Soviet Union with no state religions certainly want fealty to their secular authority which otherwise attracts harsh punishment if not death as in Myanmar (Burma) right now.

Perhaps the most influential force against reducing growth in human numbers must be the vast power of businesses whose mantras feature endless plans to grow just to meet the needs of this constant growth. More, more, more seems better and better.

And then there are us human consumers with our appetites fully stimulated for endless consumption.

Hardly a promising atmosphere for restraint.

But with Mother Nature's forces now the only enforcing limits to human numbers growth we find our new President Biden embracing climate change. At least that implies a limit to growth.

But I know of no proposed solutions to climate change that include calls for efforts to cut human numbers.

Our growing weather disasters don't elicit calls for fewer of us either.

And one would think our global pandemic might suggest a need for human numbers limitation, but I haven't heard any calls from major world leaders for fewer human numbers! Just for more vaccines and treatment equipment. New pandemics are surely predictable but losing people to disease is not a reduction method we find attractive. Or is it if we do nothing about human numbers.

Family planning is still the key path to lessening human numbers safely and humanely. There are so many methods now available which can safely bring fertility regulation to anyone who wants it. Massive further such funding is needed, but the funding for war ironically surpasses so many other priorities which would help humans. Killing our way with war to fewer won't work as we have proved often. However, nukes would certainly do the job.

So, as I recently wrote, despite urgent pleas for more family planning from NGOs such as Population

Connection and scientific voices like E.O. Wilson, the only real effective restraints on the continuing increase in human numbers has been left to the Four Horseman of the Apocalypse—variously called war, famine, pestilence, and disease—while the rich get richer and mostly ignore these burgeoning threats like those nobles in Edgar Allen Poe's classic *The Masque of the Red Death*.

It would seem, that there is no hope.

However, despite what I have written here, I believe that we are approaching a time of a great awakening. We now know, as we press outward into space, that, as Copernicus proposed and Galileo proved, we are not the center of our solar system, as we are likely not alone in the vast as yet unreachable solar systems of other stars, surrounded by many planets which look like Earth.

How can we continue to be so mindless in not dealing with limits on our tiny planet??

> "March 15, 2021
>
> Dear Don and Sally,
>
> We seek your counsel, Maestro.
>
> We have been dismayed that the population issue has vanished from environmental groups agenda the past 20 years in this country.

Our interest was sparked by the Ehrlichs' work in 1968.

We made a small gift to the Population Connection last year and have been quite impressed by what they do and where their emphasis falls.

For example, they cite, crisply and deftly:

— Population growth will be among the main challenges for development and peace.

— The least peaceful countries will have an additional 1.3 billion people and will be home to more than half of the world's population.

— There is now 60% less fresh water.

— 1% of people are responsible for half of all aviation emissions.

— Trump left International Abortion Rights in Shambles... Biden vowed to repeal the Global Gag Rule.

and so forth and so on ... stuff you already know and have written about at length.

When I ran a foundation, we poured a half a million a year into population through the Pop Counsel, Planned Parenthood, and other channels.

Do you have a clear take? Supposedly they support ZPG.

Cheers,"

Name withheld for privacy's sake.

# CHAPTER 9 REPUBLICAN PARTY RACISM COULD BRING DOWN OUR REPUBLIC

*22 February 2021*

If the Trump insurrection against our elected Presidency did not awaken all of us to the fragile nature of our democracy, events going forward under a competent President should let us know how lucky we were!

That racism still controls a significant number of Republicans remains a dangerous issue which means we must understand racism's 400 year origins so we as a nation can get past where we have been to where we must go.

My writing to date on racism has been limited to simply citing its insidious existence. American literature from James Baldwin and so many others came before the significant demographic changes that now are upon us.

Consequently, when I noted the arrival of a new book The Sum Of Us by Heather McGhee, an African American author who got as I did (in 1953—among its first grads) a BA in American Studies I got a copy and devoured the intensity and urgency for dealing with this fatal Achilles Heel in the Republican Party

You can read some reviews here.

**"Review**

"The Sum of Us is a powerhouse of a book about the deep, enduring, cross-cultural, multi-generational, and real-life cost of racist policy-making in the United States. With intelligence and care (as well as with a trove of sometimes heart-breaking and sometimes heart-opening true stories) Heather McGhee shows us what racism has cost all of us, as a society. And that cost has been brutally high, across the board. This is a book for every American, and I am grateful for McGhee's research, her humanity, and her never-more-important teachings." **—Elizabeth Gilbert, #1 New York Times bestselling author**

"In this critical moment where we have fallen so far apart, The Sum of Us is a book we all need. For close to a decade, the BlackLivesMatter movement has been doing the work to change how racism, and America's willful amnesia surrounding it, devastatingly impacts the lives of Black people in America and around the world. This book provides an important and necessary piece of the equation—not just how racism hurts Black people and people of color, but white people too. The Sum of Us is a must read for everyone who wants to understand how we got here, but more importantly, where we can go from here—and how we get there, together." —**Alicia Garza, author of The Purpose of Power and co-founder of Black Lives Matter**

"If everyone in America read this book, we'd be not only a more just country, but a more powerful, successful, and loving one.... A vital, urgent, stirring, beautifully written book that offers a compassionate road map out of our present troubled moment." —**George Saunders, #1 New York Times bestselling and Booker Prize-winning author of Lincoln in the Bardo**

"Heather McGhee does not shy away from telling hard truths. Racism sits at the heart of America, and McGhee shows its effects on the very people who cleave to it. The Sum of Us removes the cloak from this land of so-called innocents and brilliantly offers a path forward for the nation. This book is for all of us standing in the breach, working toward social change. With care and unflinching honesty, McGhee has written an extraordinary book for these difficult days." —**Eddie S. Glaude Jr., New York Times bestselling author of**

**Begin Again: James Baldwin's America and Its Urgent Lessons for Our Own**

"What would it be like to live in an America where we embraced diversity as our superpower? Heather McGhee's The Sum of Us challenges readers to imagine a country where we are more than the sum of our disparate parts. Through the stories of fast food workers in Missouri, community organizers in Maine, and more, McGhee illustrates the power and necessity of multi-racial organizing. Hopeful, inspiring, and timely, The Sum of Us makes the case for the radical notion that 'we the people' means all of us." **—Cécile Richards, co-founder, Supermajority, and former president, Planned Parenthood**

"Heather McGhee is one of the wisest, most penetrating, most brilliant minds to set herself to the Big Problem of American democracy: how we share this country in a way that works for all of us. Reading it made me feel free, truly free, and ready to run and march and shout. I think it will do the same for you." **—Chris Hayes, New York Times bestselling author and Emmy Award–winning news anchor**

> About the Author
>
> Heather McGhee is an expert in economic and social policy. The former president of the inequality-focused think tank Demos, McGhee has drafted legislation, testified before Congress and contributed regularly to news shows including NBC's Meet the Press. She now chairs the board of Color of Change, the nation's largest online racial justice organization. McGhee holds a BA in American studies from Yale University and a JD from the University of California at Berkeley School of Law."

So, to conclude, Trump, not only the supreme egotist, but the ultimate racist leader, heads millions who want to deny their racist fears and think they can still mount a national presence as a co-equal member of our two-party system.

As the growing disgust with Trump will prove, the need to change will grow more urgent.

# CHAPTER 10 TRUMP IS A POLITICAL GONER, BUT THE GOP FUTURE DEPENDS ON MCCONNELL AND OTHERS WHO MIGHT VOTE TO CONVICT HIM FOR THE GOP'S SALVATION

*6 February 2021*

With Trump's false information amplifiers gone—without Fox at whipping up frenzy and Twitter fully locked out forever from his use—Americans can now fully and clearly see that this would be racist king has no clothes!

As I have reported early and often—most recently in my 2/2/21 op ed—Trump is a goner! Now with $2.7 billion lawsuit against FOX for its comments about a voting machine maker that suit puts realistic teeth in the Trump habit of spreading false information! That BIG LIE about the 11/3/20 election must be paid for.

The now disgraced former President declined to testify at his 2/9/21 Senate trial under oath, proving that his big lie about who won the election deserves his conviction.

So, Trump is a political goner and thanks to the gutless Kevin McCarthy leadership so is the credibility of the present GOP to anyone who can listen or read the facts.

Ann Applebaum Editor of The Atlantic, appearing on WETA's 2/4/21 News Hour estimated that about 20 percent of Trump's manic supporters remain dangerously alienated. Hard to be certain.

These zealots of course need to be carefully monitored lest they plan more violence.

But these types have been around for a long time. Recall the 1995 Murrah office building bombing by Timothy McVeigh which killed 168 people and injured more than 680 others! As Wikipedia tells us,

> "Timothy James McVeigh (April 23, 1968 – June 11, 2001) was an American domestic terrorist who carried out the 1995 Oklahoma City bombing that killed 168 people and injured more than 680 others, and destroyed one third of the Alfred P. Murrah Federal Building. The bombing was the deadliest act of terrorism in the United States prior to the September 11 attacks. It remains the deadliest act of domestic terrorism in U.S. history.
>
> A Gulf War veteran, McVeigh sought revenge against the federal government for the 1993 Waco siege that ended in the deaths of 86 people, many of whom were children, as well as the 1992 Ruby Ridge incident and American foreign policy. He

hoped to inspire a revolution against the federal government, and defended the bombing as a legitimate tactic against what he saw as a tyrannical government. He was arrested shortly after the bombing and indicted on 160 state offenses and 11 federal offenses, including the use of a weapon of mass destruction. He was found guilty on all counts in 1997 and sentenced to death.

McVeigh was executed by lethal injection on June 11, 2001, at the Federal Correctional Complex in Terre Haute, Indiana. His execution was carried out in a considerably shorter time than most inmates awaiting the death penalty. Terry Nichols and Michael Fortier were convicted as conspirators in the plot. Nichols was sentenced to eight life terms for the deaths of eight federal agents, and to 161 life terms without parole by the state of Oklahoma for the deaths of the others. Michael Fortier was sentenced to 12 years' imprisonment and has since been released. Lori Fortier was given immunity in exchange for her testimony against the others."

But, Folks, as I am sure many Americans who voted for Biden, now understand completely what is so serious and what is unique about this case! Seemingly dismissed by coverup Republicans like McCarthy in the case of Charlottesville, or Trump's hour-long recorded phone call to Atlanta's Republican election officials, asking them to find 11,000 votes, and now his clear instigation of the U.S. Capitol insurrection was that these acts were willfully performed by the President of the United States.

Retired Republican House member from Philadelphia, Charlie Dent on the 2/4/21 Don Lemon program called Trump's behavior "political malpractice". I call it treason.

After her AM press conference on 2/5/21 defrocked of her House committee assignments, House member Marjorie Taylor Greene said that Trump still controls the GOP.

Many Republicans, as their voting behavior proves, now seem to believe that Trump and Marjorie Taylor Greene are far more popular than McConnell and Liz Chaney.

Greene's 2/5/21 news conference produced banal, childish, and dangerous phases like: "I was allowed to believe things that weren't true". Oh? Her humungous racism was dismissed by Marjorie Taylor Greene as "words of the past". Greene blames the media for what she said on tape and recorded. Sound familiar?

I don't believe Trump's control of the GOP will be a position which can be sustained very long.

Biden will do a competent job, even if Republicans say he spends too much. Republicans of course in the Trump years were delighted to give the rich big tax cuts and add trillions to the national debt!

Trump's administration brought America to its knees, morally and emotionally as behavioral traditions we had assumed were inviolable were replaced with hate, racism, greed and immorality at every turn.

As I watched his term unfold, I could not help but think of the decline and fall of earlier empires as our government dismissed core values, we had long treasured.

We seemed to be moving away from the institutional racism that George Floyd's murder had exemplified when all of a sudden, the party of Lincoln proved to be even more racist, tribal and corrupt with Republican leaders unwilling to make the move they did with Nixon at Watergate. We slid backwards under Trump to an unbelievable degree. This is not politics this is self-destruction.

The ridiculous argument most Republicans are hiding behind is that since Trump is out of office to convict him is unconstitutional. Highly questionable but worse highly immoral in light of Trump's behavior.

Yes, a smooth, honest, professionally competent, perhaps too liberal but very transparent Biden reign will help, but Trump is lurking, and the worst elements of our society stand ready to grab power.

So, to have a trial without a conviction will administer a stain on our democracy which will not be easily translatable into wide recognition of America's uniqueness or even to encourage our model's emulation by others.

We should not, as the spineless Republicans advise "get over this and move on".

NY Times columnist, Tom Friedman pointed out that our failure to embrace the facts of our situation will destroy our fragile democracy.

The GOP is now called by House Speaker Nancy Pelosi the Q Party! Are we ready, Mitch McConnell, to do the right thing in this upcoming acid test of our republic?

# CHAPTER 11 ARE WE AS A NATION GOING UP OR DOWN AFTER JANUARY 6TH? NOT IF MCCONNELL AND OTHERS SHOWED SOME BACKBONE

*4 February 2021*

Two face Kevin McCarthy flight to Mar Lago for his photo op on January 28 with disgraced ex-President Trump shows the January 6th attempt to overthrow Trump's lost election is still okay with some Republican leaders. McCarthy's failure to acknowledge the treasonous statements of freshman GA House member Marjorie Taylor Greene while seeking to bring down House Republican heroine Liz Cheney shows the dangerous level of fragility our democracy has reached.

The upcoming trial of Trump has much more importance than many seem to be giving it. To me it represents the opportunity which must be taken to convict a felon whose continuing legacy will be one of deception and corruption in his and his followers (Cruz and Hawley perfect examples).

As former Republican Senator Jeff Flake said in effect on CNN on 1/25 if what Trump did is not a convictable offense then what is?

It is time for the good people in our Congress on both sides of the aisle to make their mark on history as McConnell has suggested by voting their consciences.

The effect of not convicting Trump for a variety of political reasons, will empower Trump and his most evil, misguided backers with power to keep persuading those voters who believed his lies, and tried to change what was the cleanest National election in our history, with a violent assault on our Capitol on the very day the votes of our electoral college votes were being formally accepted by Congress.

This is no time to waver
This is no time for excuses
This is no time for lack of backbone

As Flake also said (and I totally agree) Trump's political influence will decline faster than people think.

I have been making this point as no legitimate business is going to want to risk alienating a majority of its customers with the stench of Trump's reputation. Will companies such as Proctor and Gamble want their customers to know they gave campaign contributions to such scumbags?

More important, will the Republican Party in the hands of Trump regain its footing?

My answer, I hope so, because our 2-party system with all its flaws gives balance for legitimate dissent and respectful resolution.

Trump's perfidy will continue to hasten his decline. My favorite sport, golf, has already acted decisively by canceling holding 2 major tournaments at Trump owned courses!

The backers of Trump are going to find it rapidly harder to win with the support from this congenital liar whose only aim is self-aggrandizement!

Watch. His political fall whether he is convicted or not is going to be rapid and spectacular.

Biden, if he can get COVID corralled, and adequate emergency funding in motion, will allow the huge resurgence of our economy to bring in a new era of prosperity.

But again, clarity and courage by Republican conviction votes would do much to remove the shame of the tragically weak performance of the Republican Party during the Trump Administration.

These elected representatives need to look in the mirror and decide to go down in history as a toady or a person of principle.

The key Republican vote is McConnell. Even if there aren't 17 Republican votes to convict Trump, the courage of McConnell's vote might make the undecided elected Republicans decide that the Trump game is over, and it is time to restore the utterly disgraced GOP image.

The bottom-line GOP flaw is the embrace of racism by the white nationalists who stormed our Capitol on January 6th. Those Republican voters who shared the view of Trump's lie about election fraud who were NOT there better wake up and agree saving our fragile democracy is worth avoiding the anarchy ominous with a Trump dominated party.

Look at what Trump left us? COVID deaths are likely to reach 600,000 before being contained.

# CHAPTER 12 ADD POTENTIAL DEATHS OF CONGRESS MEMBERS FROM MOB TO TRUMP CASE?

*3 February 2021*

The AOL headline of its story written by Eric Tucker and Mary Clare Jalonick of February 2, 2021 says "Dems: Trump aimed 'loaded cannon' of supporters at Capitol" and goes on to state the totally plausible case quoting from the trial brief to be used next week that:

> "Donald Trump endangered the lives of all members of Congress when he aimed a mob of supporters 'like a loaded cannon' at the U.S. Capitol, House Democrats said Tuesday in making their most detailed case yet for why the former president should be convicted and permanently barred from office.
>
> The legal brief forcefully links Trump's baseless efforts to overturn the results of the presidential election to the deadly Jan. 6 riot at the Capitol, saying he bears 'unmistakable' blame for actions that directly threatened the underpinnings of American democracy. It argues that he must be found guilty when his impeachment trial opens before the

> Senate next week on a charge of inciting the siege."

Then the authors quoting from the brief prepared for his case, they quote as follows:

> "His conduct endangered the life of every single Member of Congress, jeopardized the peaceful transition of power and line of succession, and compromised our national security,' the Democratic managers of the impeachment case wrote. 'This is precisely the sort of constitutional offense that warrants disqualification from federal office."

Then the authors further state that:

> "The legal brief lays out for the first time the arguments House lawmakers expect to present at the impeachment trial. It not only explicitly faults him for his role in the riot but also aims to preemptively rebut defense claims that Trump's words were somehow protected by the First Amendment or that an impeachment trial is unconstitutional, or even unnecessary, now that Trump has left office. It says Trump's behavior was so egregious as to require permanent disqualification from office.

> The Constitution specifies that disqualification from office can be a punishment for an impeachment conviction."

They continue to quote from the legal brief:

> "This is not a case where elections alone are a sufficient safeguard against future abuse; it is the electoral process itself that President Trump attacked and that must be protected from him and anyone else who would seek to mimic his behavior."

The authors then tell us that:

> "Lawyers for Trump are expected to file their own brief Tuesday. In a Fox News appearance Monday night, one of the attorneys, David Schoen, said he would argue that the trial was unconstitutional, that efforts to bar Trump from office were undemocratic. and that his words were protected by the First Amendment.
>
> Democrats made clear that they disagree with all points."

Again, from the Democrats' brief:

> "The only honorable path at that point was for President Trump to accept

the results and concede his electoral defeat. Instead, he summoned a mob to Washington, exhorted them into a frenzy, and aimed them like a loaded cannon down Pennsylvania Avenue,' they wrote in their 77-page brief.

The Democrats draw heavily on the words of prominent Republicans who have criticized the former president, including Wyoming. Rep. Liz Cheney, who voted for his impeachment and said there has never been a 'greater betrayal' by a president, and Senate Republican Leader Mitch McConnell, who said Trump 'provoked' the rioters.

Still, Republicans have signaled that acquittal is likely, with many saying they think Congress should move on and questioning the constitutionality of an impeachment trial — Trump's second — now that he has left office. In a test vote in the Senate last week, 45 Republicans voted in favor of an effort to dismiss the trial over those constitutional concerns.

Though no president has been tried after departing the White House, Democrats say there is precedent, pointing to an 1876 impeachment of a secretary of war who resigned his office in a last-ditch attempt

> to avoid an impeachment trial. The Senate held it anyway.
>
> The Democrats write that the framers of the Constitution would not have wanted to leave the country defenseless against 'a president's treachery in his final days, allowing him to misuse power, violate his Oath, and incite insurrection against Congress and our electoral institutions' simply because he is leaving office. Setting that precedent now would 'horrify the Framers,' the brief says.
>
> 'There is no "January Exception" to impeachment or any other provision of the Constitution,' the Democrats wrote. 'A president must answer comprehensively for his conduct in office from his first day in office through his last."

As the authors remind us, "Trump was impeached by the House while still in office, they note, forcing a Senate trial. And there are precedents for trying former officials."

Then reminding us about the dispute widely used by Republicans that the trial is unconstitutional the authors again quote from the legal brief, "Trump is personally responsible for a violent attack on the Capitol, he was impeached while still in office. The case for trying him after he has left office is stronger than any of the precedents."

At this point it is important to remind readers that early on, on Tuesday, January 12th, a conservative House leader Rep. Liz Cheney (R-Wyo.), the chair of the House Republican conference said she would (and did) vote to impeach President Donald Trump for his role in the previous week's brutal assault on the Capitol, alleging he "summoned this mob, assembled the mob, and lit the flame of this attack."

Lest we fail to note other examples of political courage in sticking to the oaths they took to uphold in office, these Republicans deserve our thanks.

Willing to vote for Trump's removal are Sen. Lisa Murkowski (R-Alaska), Sen. Pat Toomey (R-Pa.) and Utah Senator Mitt Romney. Reps. Peter Meijer (R-Mich.) and Adam Kinzinger (R-Ill.), the latter already voted for Trump's impeachment.

Now, after telling his colleagues to vote their consciences, how is Senator Mitch McConnell going to vote? He is no fan of Trump and should see Trump's political demise as hugely beneficial to the GOP's recovery.

# CHAPTER 13 VETERAN WSJ COLUMNIST PEGGY NOONAN VOTES IN HER 1/28/21 OP-ED TO CONVICT TRUMP

*1 February 2021*

The lead editorial in the 1/30/21 WSJ by Peggy Noonan "Rob Portman's Exit Interview" lauds his moderate balanced eleven year Senate record as he plans to retire at the end of his term in 2021.

Only 65 Portman says he's tired of seeing nothing getting done legislatively. As for the upcoming Trump trial in the Senate, Portman says he "will listen to both sides, and I will. I'm a juror". But then Noonan tells us Portman says he "believes trying a former President sees a bad precedent"!

The main cop out Republican excuse for not convicting Trump is that it is unconstitutional since he is no longer President. There are many legal opinions which differ with that view, as Republican Senator Mitt Romney who will vote to convict, argued. Senator Romney one of the few Republican Senators who will vote to convict notes that if what Trump did is not convictable, what is?

Noonan is eloquent in using her contacts with foreign observers and others to make an overlooked aspect of not convicting the villainous Trump as it might be perceived by democratic foreign observers.

As Noonan says:

> "I started the new year talking with an ambassador to the U.S. from a European nation, who spoke of Mr. Trump's campaign to delegitimize the election. Do Americans understand the damage this does to U.S. allies, the ambassador asked. We look to you for an example of how to do democracy—you're the oldest in the world! It grieves us to see the beacon of democracy sullied in this way.
>
> Those words rang in my ears five days later as I watched the Capitol besieged.
>
> On "Axios on HBO" Sunday we will hear from President Volodymyr Zelensky of Ukraine. He is playing a hard hand. Russia is breathing down his neck, Republicans don't want to hear about him because they're embarrassed by the Trump phone call that triggered the first impeachment, and Democrats are embarrassed by Hunter Biden and Burisma. Mr. Zelensky seems kind of on his own, sitting on top of one of the world's flashpoints. China has been sweetly reaching out.

Reporter Jonathan Swan asked the president how he felt as he saw the Capitol stormed. "Shocked," Mr. Zelensky said. "I could not even imagine something like this was possible in the United States of America. … We are used to thinking that the U.S. has ideal democratic institutions where power is passed calmly, without war, without revolutions." Such things happen elsewhere; they've happened in Ukraine. "That it could happen in the United States, no one expected that. … After something like this, I believe it would be very difficult for the world to see the United States as a symbol of democracy in the world."

For more than a century we have claimed the mantle of world power, basked in the warm glow of our exceptionalism, and put ourselves forward as an example. When you do that you have responsibilities; you owe something in return. What you owe is the kind of admirable behavior that gives the world something to aim for. On 1/6 they saw the storming and the siege and thought: Ah, no stability in that place. We can't learn how to do it there and replicate it here.

This is a loss to rising democracies and also to us, to our standing and reputation.

> Senate conviction is the chance to show the world: No, we won't have this; those who did it will pay the highest penalty.
>
> It matters that all evidence be presented, that everyone sees we can come down like a hammer, ensuring that 1/6 was a regrettable incident, not a coming tendency.
>
> It matters that the world see this. That we see it."

You can read the entire piece here.

On CNN on 1/29 on Don Lemon's late-night program, pundit Paul Begala reminded us about how his Democrat Party had harbored the Ku Klux Klan for decades but now the Republican Party had taken the racist banner symbolized by Trump and instead of taking the chance of putting Trump aside Kevin McCarthy and others continue to kiss Trump's ring which can only lead to not winning national elections and losing for years.

The 2022 election will be the next major test. I predict Trump influence will be minimal by then as Biden's record of competence will satisfy many voters not hyped on fantasies!

# CHAPTER 14 HENRY AARON'S LIFE STORY OFFERS A HUGE EXAMPLE TO THE GOP TO EMBRACE RACIAL EQUITY

*22 January 2021*

The page one stories with photos in the January 23rd Wall Street Journal and the Washington Post and the lengthy stories inside told poignant stories about baseball legend Henry Aaron's life, a baseball career of triumph against his suffering severe racial bias. You can read the WSJ story with its moving photos and comments here.

In 1974 after he beat Babe Ruth's record with 714 home runs while playing in Atlanta, he found it brought threats of death which required him to have a bodyguard for years in Atlanta. As he continued to set his peerless home run record and other stats the racism against him should make us all cringe with regret, but his quiet civil rights record gained him accolades from many key leaders later.

The Biden cabinet appointment of black General Austin to head DOD and other black luminaries should further notify the GOP that its racial bias as symbolized by the Trump instigated attack on our Capitol will lead it into a one-way decline to permanent minority or extinction.

Trump's threat to form a new party if convicted seems even more outlandish as the prosecution of those involved in the Capitol invasion escalates.

But by no means should we dismiss the chance for dangerous further violence from these anti-constitutional government felons. We can hope that Biden's performance in his first 100 days (curbing COVID-19 primary goal!) will be highly influential in restoring majority citizen confidence that we can right our listing ship of state!

But let's really be sure the symbolism offered by the peerless examples of black men and women such as Henry Aaron, Martin Luther King, John Lewis and Rosa Parks carry both parties to a new level of racial justice.

My January 22 op ed suggested that the upcoming trial of ex-President Trump gives the GOP a perfect chance to begin to put Trump in its rearview mirror.

Whether the GOP takes that opportunity remains to be seen as hardcore pro Trump representatives such as Jim Jordan will continue to try to intimidate.

However, the agreement yesterday to postpone the Senate trial's beginning until February 9 seems to be a good compromise for both parties as it gives Biden time to get his key administration's nominations confirmed and perhaps even some agreement on his economic aid package now under questioning from members of both parties.

McConnell now has more time to seek more anti-Trump votes for conviction, but realistically veteran NY Times columnist such as David Brooks and many pundits see little chance for Mitch rounding up 16 Republican senators to join him in convicting Trump, even if he decided to vote for conviction which he has not said he would.

Evidence continues to mount about Trump's scandalous behavior which will continue to diminish his political future. Still to not gain a conviction leaves undetermined who controls the GOP. I don't think the stench of racism, once clear to more and more voters, will help the GOP.

Evolution from such deep seeded racism going back to the Civil War has taken time but the election of two Democratic senators from Georgia was proof of Trump's diminishment.

And the Washington Post article on Mr. Henry Aaron gives us hope that residual institutional racism is waning. I think you will enjoy reading here the piece entitled "Henry Aaron did as much as anyone to redeem the South".

# CHAPTER 15 TRUMP'S GOP OR MCCONNELL'S GOP? IT DEPENDS ON CONVICTION OR NOT!

*22 January 2021*

The headline news today is that the Senate will receive Trump's impeachment document from the House of Representatives on Monday, January 25th, which will immediately initiate Trump's trial, some days before McConnell had requested its start on February 11th. What effect this will have on the vote to convict is uncertain, but key to there being 17 Republican votes to add to the 50 Democratic votes will be whether or not McConnell votes to convict.

As you know, January 17th marked Martin Luther King's birthday. In marking MLK's day, we can pause to calibrate where we stand as a nation on the obviously unsolved issue of racism.

In my view, the majority of Americans have already decided that ethnicity should not destroy the world's greatest democracy.

Sadly, the record shows that many GOP elected members of the U.S. Congress have not come to that recognition. Yes, arguing about excess immigration as the reason for taking American jobs is a factor to resolve, but we have not used as another reason.

Those members who have not decided are likely playing to their constituents out of their own fear of not being reelected, or perhaps attacked by the extremist types who attacked our Capitol, or sadly their own personal racial prejudices.

They are entitled to their own opinions, but those opinions will not prevail as the majority in the upcoming trial of Donald Trump, even if 67 total votes in the Senate for conviction cannot be achieved.

As noted above, Mitch McConnell is likely to be the key to Trump's conviction, not because the long time Senate Minority Leader has come 180 degrees on his views of race, but because he knows the key to resurrecting his party must begin with the conviction of Trump.

This view was buttressed by the 1/22 op ed by now U.S. citizen the former Soviet chess champion, Garry Kasporov, in the Wall Street Journal which you can read here.

Trump's life history has come to be so heinously disreputable and now capped with his role in fostering the January 6th Capitol assault. Senator McConnell is certainly not alone in either party in knowing that the time has come for action on the charge that Trump committed convictable offenses far too serious to be ignored if any GOP credibility is to be restored.

On 1/20 the Wall Street Journal writer Lindsay Wise and 2 other WSJ writers updated what they wrote, "On Tuesday, Senate Majority Leader Mitch McConnell said President

Trump provoked the mob that attacked the Capitol on Jan. 6 and spoke of moving the country forward." You can read his views here.

Where stood those 140 Republican House members when the Trump's House impeachment trial was being voted on? Voting for Trump's acquittal of course.

Not all sitting Republican House members were so minded.

As Peggy Noonan's January 14th WSJ column told us, "Liz Cheney's was a moment of real stature. Addressing the issue of impeachment, the third-ranking member of the Republican leadership said, of the events of Jan. 6: "The president of the United States summoned this mob, assembled the mob, and lit the flame of this attack. Everything that followed was his doing. None of this would have happened without the president. The president could have immediately and forcefully intervened to stop the violence. He did not. There has never been a greater betrayal by a president of the United States of his office and his oath to the Constitution."

Noonan continues, "And so she would vote to impeach. Her remarks implicitly urged others in her party to do so, and the bluntness and power of what she said offered them cover: They could be tough too. But most couldn't. They were stupid and cowardly."

You can read her entire column here.

But Trump's conviction would add powerful recognition about our recovery as a nation from the overt racism which has plagued us since the Civil War. Thus, to begin to restore the balance to our two-party system, the need for a Trump conviction looms large.

So, regardless of motivation, I hope that McConnell will rise to the occasion and vote to convict. McConnell surely knows that a conviction vote will mark him in history with the vast majority of Americans as a hero. Moreover, his vote to convict would no doubt be influential in possibly encouraging conviction votes from the 16 other Republican Senators whose votes will be required to make conviction happen!

Trump said that if convicted he will start his own party, but as I have predicted, Trump's political clout balloon is deflating daily and his attraction even to his most faithful fans will be less persuasive as time passes.

Read about his new party intentions here.

Perhaps his greatest conviction will come as he begins to resume his post Presidency life as his brand gets a negative branding which this piece in the Washington Post describes.

# CHAPTER 16 TRUMP ECHOES CIVIL WAR ERA RACISM! CONVICT HIM!

*18 January 2021*

For many white middleclass moderates like me the May 25, 2020, murder of George Floyd in Minneapolis was a sharp wake up call. I had assumed, as the number of prominent African Americans flourished in our public life, the presence of racial bias was fading away! My bad!

How wrong I could have been was one of the many lessons brought home to me and I hope to many Americans by the Capitol attack on January 6th, a day certain to live in infamy like December 7th when the Japanese attacked Pearl Harbor, except these January 6th attackers were American citizens.

One key aspect of this Trump insurrection was greatly illuminated for me by the historic truths set forth in her January 17th Washington Post article entitled "The Lost Cause" by Professor of history Karen L Cox at UNC whose book "No Common Ground: Confederate Monuments and the Ongoing Fight For Social Justice". I listed the 5 Myths she articulates below, but you can read her facts by going to her full article here.

Myth No. 1
**The Civil War was not fought over slavery.**

Myth No. 2
**The South lost simply because the North had more resources.**
Myth No. 3
**Robert E. Lee abhorred slavery.**
Myth No. 4
**Confederate monuments only recently became controversial.**
Myth No. 5
**Removing a Confederate monument is erasing history.**

These myths, in an almost eerie way, seem to tie directly into the kind of mythology perpetrated by our outgoing President in his efforts to overthrow our constitutional democracy. Months of lying after Biden's victory on November 3rd has turned Trump's backers into a cult of deniers, unable to free themselves from a religious like belief in his lies.

Trump's backers are in effect his slaves, willing to believe and behave irrationally.

After all the slavery era in the South provides us with a mirror image of the kind of control Trump was seeking and which his obtaining a second term might have gone a long way toward his getting!

Be sure to ponder the point of my January 9th op ed about how lucky we are to now have the chance to mark Trump's immensely traitorous perfidy by gaining his conviction in the upcoming Senate trial. You can read that piece again here.

Long time Majority Speaker Mitch McConnell must be keenly aware that his image in history now rests with his vote to impeach Trump.

Not really too hard as McConnell's wife, Elaine Chao, in resigning her cabinet post after the Capitol insurrection, has already led the way.

The stench of Trump's misdeeds is now growing so rapidly that those Republicans in both Senate and House know for certain the huge eviscerating effect Trump's behavior will have on the GOP's future. I am not counting on their exercising principled behavior in voting to convict Trump in his Senate trial after their behavior for the past 4 years in letting Trump take them over. Just revenge.

Note Trump's success in making the GOP the minority party likely unable to win a national election for some time. The Republicans in both House and Senate are angry of course, but the proper vote to convict Trump could be judged by history as one of conscience for all Senators.

Historic days are ahead but the powerful symbolism of the George Floyd murder which finally awakened the recognition in so many white Americans of the deeply continuing pervasive racism—particularly and so ironically in the Party of Lincoln—gives all Americans a great opportunity to enhance our image on the world stage, an image so jeopardized by Trump's disastrous behavior.

Most commentators expect Trump to continue to wield huge power after he leaves office. I disagree with those observers, because as the stench of his personal life, his lies, and worse, the endangerment of our constitutional government, come to be more and more understood, and daily reiterated by our media at all levels, he is going to be like a deflating balloon, pursued by his creditors, and shunned by most of his November 3, 2020, voters.

Americans—most of us—who are not afflicted with Trump's egotistical mania and can still be reached with facts are increasingly, as they should be, upset with the implications of what Trump caused. No armed march which was expected on Sunday, January 17th (Ben Franklin's birthday) happened as this 1/18 Washington Post piece describes but the majority of us are not going to stand for this situation. Read the whole piece here.

Watch in the days ahead as real patriots take issue with his treason and as Trump's power balloon keeps deflating! We as a republic are not going back to the racist days of the post Reconstruction era even if some in the GOP would like us to.

# CHAPTER 17 AMERICA WAS LUCKY IF WE GET WHAT HAPPENED ON JANUARY 6$^{TH}$ AND ACT

*15 January 2021*

Like all of us except the conspirators, I have been stunned by the events of January 6$^{th}$ and its subsequent developments. As I wrote in my January 9$^{th}$ op ed:

> "First let me say that a message needs strongly made about what happened on January 6$^{th}$.
>
> Secondly, while what happened was terrible, this historic occurrence was sadly required to bring more Americans to the realization of what Trump caused with his conduct.
>
> Had Trump left before Wednesday's example his call to Georgia's Atty General demanding him to "find the votes" to overturn Biden's November 3$^{rd}$ win might have been forgotten by too many and as was blatantly disregarded and used for political gain by Ted Cruz and Josh Hawley.

> Please don't give me that lame excuse that we are out of time for action now so why bother!!
>
> If the GOP wants to go the way of the WHIGS in the 1850 lead up to the Civil War, let them resist Trump's total censure!"

Where has Trump left America after packing the Supreme Court and 4 years of dangerous mismanagement?

I say in luck if we are now able to right our ship of state because of fully recognizing the effect of two unforeseen events.

1. The horrible pandemic for which our amazing private sector has produced vaccines in record time.
2. The attack Trump fostered and precipitated on our Capitol on January 6th.

Otherwise, horrible as those events were and still are, Trump's reelection this past November 3rd would have been assured and the possible end to our constitutional democracy could have gotten so well advanced that we could not have recovered.

The psychosis of today's America in letting Trump not be convicted of impeachable behavior could come as it did with Germany at about the time of my birth in 1931 from many sources some beautifully described in the attached Scientific American article which you can read here.

A large number of elected members of the Republican Party don't want to admit their mistake with Trump as many feel he was good for business.

In fact, as this seminal debate on impeachment occurred on January 13th in the House, the CNBC investment channel was far more engaged in how stocks were heading than whether Trump would continue to dominate the Republican future.

Everyone in Congress admits that the Capitol invasion was bad, but Trump initially seemed to get a pass on culpability from far too many Republicans in both houses.

Is it greed or reach for power such as Cruz appears to have sought?

Did not getting re-elected move so many? Doubtless.

But also, many comments being expressed now and confirmed by the FBI was their fear of being physically endangered by the kind of far-right leaders of the Capitol invasion that urged their supporters to hang Pence or murder Pelosi!

By the way, this abject failure to early on call out Hitler by the moderates of that time was what ultimately brought the Third Reich to full power.

Trump needs to be called to harsh account now. His delay on recognizing COVID was a minor mistake compared to what is brewing if his lying Roger Stone origins as so powerfully depicted in the Tuesday January 12th Frontline program on WETA.

I was shocked that the Washington Post and other reputable media did not mention Frontline's searing accounting of how lying got Trump elected. You can find that program here.

So, after all these factual disclosures, we still have over 100 Republican members of the U.S. House and who knows how many in the Senate, willing to not impeach a traitor to our Republic.

Why, obviously because of their fear of personal harm or their political future, both sad and dangerous for our future.

I am a fervent backer of our two-party system, but the only way the Republican Party can regain its balance is the get the stench of Trump off its back. I am not a Mitch McConnell fan, but his early recognition of Trump's impact on his party has left the door open for the less brave of his tribe when impeachment surfaces again either immediately or after Biden has a chance to get his administration off to a needed start.

The reaction of big business which was happy to take Trump's goodies is not clear; they see the profit loss danger of not getting rid of him. His brand is going to symbolize the tyranny of his totally self-interested objectives and his failure to admit culpability for his clearly traitorous behavior.

Watch as this behavior gains more and more recognition from Republicans on the right, whose behavior is clearly motivated at least partially by racism as Don Lemon so clearly explains on his CNN 11PM talk show.

Wonder what will happen on January 20th in all the 50 state capitals?

# CHAPTER 18 THIS TRUMP EXIT NEEDS SHARPLY MARKED WITH AN IMPEACHMENT

*9 January 2021*

First, let me say that a message needs strongly made about what happened on January 6$^{th}$.

Secondly, while what happened was terrible, this historic occurrence was sadly required to bring more Americans to the realization of what Trump caused with his conduct.

Had Trump left before Wednesday's example his call to Georgia's Atty General demanding him to "find the votes" to overturn Biden's November 3$^{rd}$ win might have been forgotten by too many, and as was blatantly disregarded, and used for political gain by Ted Cruz and Josh Hawley.

Please don't give me that lame excuse that we are out of time for action now so why bother!!

If the GOP wants to go the way of the WHIGS in the 1850 lead up to the Civil War, let them resist Trump's total censure!

The Washington Post lead editorial reflected my view of the events of Jan 6$^{th}$ but I went also to the Saturday January 9, 2021 Wall Street Journal op ed section and found its leading editorialist Peggy Noonan in agreement.

You can read the Post's lead here.

Noonan's final paragraph:

> "Again, on the president: There have been leaders before who, facing imminent downfall, decide to tear everything down with them. They want to go out surrounded by flames. Hitler, at the end, wanted to blow up Germany, its buildings and bridges. His people had let him down. Now he hated them. They must suffer.
>
> I have resisted Nazi comparisons for five years, for the most part easily. But that is like what is happening here, the same kind of spirit, as the president departs, as he angrily channel-surfs in his bunker.
>
> He is a bad man and not a stable one and he is dangerous. America is not safe in his hands.
>
> It is not too late. Removal of the president would be the prudent move, not the wild one. Get rid of him. Now."

You can read Noonan's entire piece here.

This vicious man's dangerous tenure must not pass without strong action which the House's expected impeachment of Trump next Wednesday the 13th would be.

That a senate conviction is not likely before Jan 20th need not keep conviction from not happening after he leaves office when control shifts to the Democrats.

One reason this might not happen is a huge and justifiable Republican fear of Trump's causing the GOP such huge and permanent embarrassment which can't be avoided anyway.

We must make a mark here for the future!

And also fix with future rules the outrageous pardons and the worst outcome which would be Trump's likely pardoning of himself!

These few days and beyond offer urgent opportunities to make points for future improvements.

Biden will be wise to concentrate on setting up his administration and focusing on stemming the raging pandemic which Trump has ignored.

But the absence of an impeachment, as I suggested in an earlier op ed would underline Trump's history over 4 years of his utter disrespect for our laws which finally culminated his continuous urging his fanatic followers to do a coup despite no proof of any fraud!

What happened last Wednesday made clear his attempt at a seditious coup.

This was a mob trying to take steps which were urged by the President of the United States amidst our worsening ongoing pandemic.

Trump stopped being President long ago and became like a would-be Mussolini or a mafia mob boss.

I listened with particular interest when General John Kelly, former Trump Chief of Staff, phoned Jake Tepper of CNN the day after the Capitol invasion on January 6$^{th}$.

In a very enlightening interview, Kelly said Trump had become a laughingstock and that he is isolated probably without much power in The White House.

Afterwards, during that day, calls for Trump's ouster escalated as images of the invasion escalated.

Guess, whether ouster happens or not, who got really embarrassed? Everyone, particularly Congress.

If the House of Representatives does impeach him, one motivating factor, likely very unstated, will be the institutional embarrassment.

A major motivator of everyone's embarrassment has to be the reactions of the international community and the mass media here that finally piqued action not the high and mighty ethics that long since should have ousted this despicable demagogue.

Perhaps no Congressional action will be quick enough before Trump pardons himself!

The chances before to get rid of Trump were many but the big money got happy with his endless obeisance to their interests while he snookered the mostly white poor into believing he was their champion even claiming on January 6th he would March with them to the Capitol.

Then when great adverse reactions to the January 6th Capitol invasion became evident (after Trump saying he loved those he had exhorted to do the invasion), he flip flopped on his beloved invaders and issued a peaceful transfer of power statement claiming (an utter lie) that he had summoned the National Guard as the terrorists got into the Capitol!

Trump probably won't be ousted but regardless there will be no small measure of embarrassment about the clear dereliction of duty on both sides of the aisle (although clearly much more Republican) that brought those thinly veiled hoots of derision from international observers.

Putin had the best laugh of all of course!

Yes, thank goodness our constitutional democracy prevails.

Let's hope Trump will get his due stamp of disapproval but be sure to understand that for all the other reasons to ouster him there is yet one likely unspoken major reason—institutional embarrassment.

And that embarrassment came like a thunderclap when in one day evident that many nations of the world were laughing not only at Trump but at the Congress which had tolerated his outrageous behavior too long.

Can they act now???

# CHAPTER 19 ON JANUARY 6TH 2021 DONALD TRUMP EXPLODED. HE IS POLITICALLY DONE BUT STILL PRESIDENT

*7 January 2021*

Yesterday was stark and almost seemed like a movie of fantasy such as the Manchurian Candidate. Fortunately, the outcome of confirming Biden's election was delayed but then confirmed by Congress many hours later.

The Trump inspired mob rushed the Capitol and entered the chambers of both houses while our elected representatives including the presiding Vice President of the United States in the Senate were hastily taken to secure places lest they be attacked by the mob.

One demonstrator was shot and killed, but the threat of curfew arrest was ignored after 6 PM. These Trump insurrectionists were treated differently than those who earlier peacefully marched for Black Lives Matter.

There are 14 dangerous days left in this demagogue's Presidency and most Americans now wonder what price Trump will pay for his lying and attempt to remain in power.

Another real question: Is he insane?

What will our elected officials now do? It is likely too late for impeachment and conviction and for invoking the 25th Amendment.

The January 7th lead editorial in the Wall Street Journal entitled The Disgrace on Capitol Hill concluded by saying,

> "Mr. Biden will become President at noon on Jan. 20, and until then the police need to restore order with as much force as necessary. [I might ask why not before?] Republicans especially need to speak against trespass and violence. As for Mr. Trump, to steal some famous words deployed in 1940 against Neville Chamberlain: "In the name of God, go."

The Disgrace on Capitol Hill "As for Mr. Trump, to steal some famous words deployed in 1940 against Neville Chamberlain: 'In the name of God, go.'" #Trump #TrumpRally #CapitolHill https://t.co/JicNMtuRpj

— Steve Rosenbush (@Steve_Rosenbush) January 7, 2021

The huge world press reaction to this event about the Shining City on The Hill was vivid and disheartening.

Why no impeachment and conviction? My earlier op ed suggested such impeachment was long overdue but this latest disrespect for our laws and his continuous urging a coup despite no proof of any fraud!

What happened yesterday made clear that Trump's hour-long importuning of the mob was another attempt at a seditious coup. He failed to march as he promised (how many promises has he lied about?) with his mob; maybe he forgot his bible.

This was, don't forget, a mob trying to take steps which were urged by the President of the United States amidst the ongoing pandemic which his indifferent handling has helped cause over 300,000 American deaths.

Trump stopped being President long ago and would have become a Mussolini or a mafia mob boss if he hadn't been stopped, but saying our system worked is not enough. And how about the disgraceful pardons? Will he now pardon himself?

What will our elected officials now do? I anxiously await justice of some legal kind. What can that be?

Watch @robertmooreitv's report from inside the Capitol building as the extraordinary events unfolded in Washington DChttps://t.co/krCQf1uQbx pic.twitter.com/SiWbzF5Nzs

— ITV News (@itvnews) January 6, 2021

# CHAPTER 20 TRUMP WON'T RESIGN, BUT HE SHOULD BE IMPEACHED AND CONVICTED NOW!!

*4 January 2021*

Far better writers than I have already stated the case proposed in my title, but without stating it, as with only 16 days to go perhaps some feel why bother?

Trying to kill our constitutional democracy with an attempt at an authoritarian coup is behavior worth the bother!

Let's see what kind of reaction comes this week from both parties and the media.

In my view Trump's call to Raffensperger should cause his immediate impeachment and conviction even though Trump is only 16 days from his exit!

The hourlong tape obtained by the Washington Post, run endlessly on tv yesterday was page one on its 1/4/21 front page today as follows:

> "President Trump urged fellow Republican Brad Raffensperger, the Georgia secretary of state, to "find" enough votes to overturn his defeat in an extraordinary one-hour phone call Saturday that legal scholars

> described as a flagrant abuse of power and a potential criminal act.
>
> The Washington Post obtained a recording of the conversation in which Trump alternately berated Raffensperger, tried to flatter him, begged him to act and threatened him with vague criminal consequences if the secretary of state refused to pursue his false claims, at one point warning that Raffensperger was taking "a big risk."
>
> Throughout the call, Raffensperger and his office's general counsel rejected Trump's assertions, explaining that the president is relying on debunked conspiracy theories and that President-elect Joe Biden's 11,779-vote victory in Georgia was fair and accurate."

The full story is here.

Then veteran columnist, WP's Dan Balz, wrote right under the WP story a piece which I can't improve on, except to hope for immediate efforts to implement the suggestion, in my title.

> "There are but 16 days left in President Trump's term, but there is no doubt that he will use all of his remaining time in office to inflict as much damage as he

can on democracy — with members of a now-divided Republican Party acting as enablers.

That there are no limits to the lengths to which he will go in this ruinous effort was made clear from a phone call he made Saturday to Georgia Secretary of State Brad Raffensperger. In the call, Trump repeatedly urged Raffensperger to "find" enough votes to allow the secretary to recalculate the election results to show that the president, rather than President-elect Joe Biden, won the state.

The call, an audio recording of which was obtained by The Washington Post's Amy Gardner, was as outrageous as it was chilling. Legal experts can debate how close to the line Trump was with the telephone call. Others can speculate about the president's current state of mind. The content of the call speaks for itself, and the audio excerpts should be heard by anyone who cares about the integrity of elections in America.

Here was a desperate president alternately begging, pleading, cajoling and, yes, seeming to threaten a state official — and fellow Republican — by asking for a change in the outcome of an election

> that already had been recounted and then certified."

Again you can read the entire piece here.

Then conservative columnist Michael Gerson weighs in with the same message and others call for strong action against those Republican Senators and House members who failed to stop the spread of these outrageous allegations, but in fact are still standing up for them.

Here's one you can read which sharply admonishes those who took Trump's false allegations: It's impeachable. It's likely illegal. It's a coup.

The deep split in the GOP is evident and now we can determine who its good guys and gals are (e.g., Romney and Cheney on the issue of Trump's culpability) when we move into the election in Georgia this week.

At least Richard Nixon had enough sense of honor to resign. Trump has no sense of honor. As I predicted in my earlier op ed, many will now see this fact and perhaps want to retrieve the GOP or even find a new political party with some sense of honor.

# CHAPTER 21 IS THE MANCHURIAN PRESIDENT DEPARTING?

*22 December 2020*

The behavior of the departing President has jogged so many into raising the question of my title that I can not make claim to originality or accuracy to any speculations I may make in this piece.

You doubtless can recall that original 1962 movie The Manchurian Candidate with Frank Sinatra has a former prisoner of war being brainwashed as an unwitting assassin for an international Communist conspiracy.

The behavior of our exiting executive so reminded the press of that movie that a myriad of pieces have appeared claiming his possible Russian perfidy.

One author of a book making that claim is a former FBI officer about which the Washington Post ran this column.

Then on December 7th Foreign Affairs columnist Tony Burman for the Toronto Star was blunt with his headline, "Donald Trump is the Manchurian president" as he opens by writing,

> "What will Americans do when it is proven to them that their president has been compromised by their most

> dangerous foreign adversary in crucial ways for more than a decade — including the bailing out of his once-bankrupt business empire with illegal Russian money, his involvement in personal and business scandals kept secret from the U.S. public but known and encouraged by the Russian government and intelligence agencies, and the rigging of the narrowly won 2016 presidential election to favour his candidacy and sabotage his Democratic opponent, with the full knowledge and complicity of the candidate, his family and senior Republican campaign team?"

You can read all of his excellent column here.

Of course the proof of his fealty for Putin and the Russians seems undoubted. So really what proof is needed beyond Trump's behavior?

Burman and many others have put sadly disturbing facts before us only to have such suspicions be ignored by over 74 million American voters, but fortunately at least considered by 81 million Americans. Let me remind my readers of another piece I wrote on August 26, "Covid-19 May Save Our Democracy".

I point out our luck in avoiding what would have doubtless been a disastrous 2nd Trump term, but of course based on a terrible price, the pandemic. In that regard, perhaps you will want to read my August 26, 2020, piece again.

Remember Michael Cohen's exposé on Trump, "Disloyal: A Memoir" came out on September 8th and Bob Woodward's "Rage" on September 15th, both apparently ignored as important by so many. Sadly, Trump has also ended by packing the Supreme Court.

Keeping our democracy moving in the right direction will not be easy. It never has been, but now with world human numbers so large, it will be under more and more pressure. At my age I worry for my younger family members who have their work cut out for them.

As my August 26th OP ED concluded:

> "The world's humans now number almost 8 billion, up from 2 billion at my birth in 1931 with many more people impacted more acutely than us around our overcrowded planet.
>
> In case people think my earlier de-growth messages about our planet's incapacity to handle that number peacefully and democratically are no longer urgently in need of recognition and action, the current climactic events worldwide should disabuse them of that illusion. I hear nothing from the Trump side except their bloated claims of how great he has made things in his tenure."

Democracies are fragile and this Trump tenure offers more proof than ever before!

# CHAPTER 22 TRUMP GETS PROFESSIONALLY ANALYZED AS UNFIT FOR OFFICE

*7 December 2020*

A key advisor, Dr. Jerrold Post, to President Jimmy Carter in giving him the psychological insights to successfully negotiate the key 1979 peace accord between Egypt's Sadat and Israel's Begin died of COVID 19 on November 22nd but not before leaving us a cogent professional psychiatric opinion on Donald Trump in a 2019 book entitled "Dangerous Charisma", co-authored with Stephanie Doucette.

President Carter recently gave Post accolades for his assistance in helping him achieve the Mideast peace accords. Carter "basically said 'I spent two weeks with these men and I wouldn't change a word of [Post's] assessments.'"

Post's life story, chronicled perfectly in the Washington Post's 12/6/20 Metro section by Sydney Trent, can be read in full here.

Trent deserves an accolade for this splendid piece about a truly Renaissance Man. You can email her your appreciation here. Sydney.Trent@washpost.com.

But in this final book "Dangerous Charisma" the authors give us perhaps the most illuminating analysis of Trump yet offered.

As Trent reports, in a December 2019 interview Post said, "The dangerous, destructive charismatic leader polarizes and identifies an outside enemy and pulls his followers together by manipulating their common feelings of victimization."

Were he to lose the election, Post said a year ago, "I think we can be assured that he will not concede early. Trump may not even recognize the legitimacy of the election."

Sadly, as Trent tells us, "After the book's publication, Post's health took a downward turn. His kidneys had already been failing, forcing him to go for dialysis several times a week, when he suffered a stroke in July. After several months in a rehabilitation facility, Post spent his final weeks of life surrounded by family at home. On Sunday Nov. 15, he began having trouble breathing. Carolyn called 911 and an ambulance rushed him to the hospital, where he tested positive for the coronavirus. He died exactly one week later."

With far too little recognition for this preceptive genius in my view.

My recent piece on a possible Trump role in the assassination of Iran's nuclear chief, received many comments in agreement including this one:

> "As far as we know — yes. It seems Trump's modus operandi is to kill as many people as he can before leaving office since he has the legal power to do so — and he is determined to make the most of it while he can exert power.
>
> Now he's decided that one of the most important things he can do is to ramp up the killings of everyone on death row — and ensure that they are executed in the most heinous way possible (for no reason except to exert his power).
>
> The people Trump admires the most and has tried to befriend are the dictators of the world. He's been studying the way the Nazis killed their victims — and he's getting excited to do the same — to change the form of execution to the worst. Trump is the white supremacist, and everyone else deserves to die if he has the power to do it. Similar to someone?"

You can read my prior op ed piece again here.

Will any of the 74 million who voted for Trump be swayed in the future by this canny Jerrold Post analysis?

How about the Republicans who gave Trump control of their party? You may recall my piece on that subject.

We may get answers after a competent government takes office in January so see if any Republicans in Congress step up to help repair the damage Trump has wrought.

But Jerrold Post's little marked legacy stands tall as a beacon of truth caught in the brambles of lies still spilling from the mouths of Trump and his doxies.

# CHAPTER 23 WAS TRUMP BEHIND THE INSANE ASSASSINATION OF IRAN'S NUCLEAR CHIEF?

*4 December 2020*

The behavior of Trump in taking steps to hamper the Biden transition opens a unique chapter in American history which goes back to the founding of our republic and the Presidency of George Washington. The word insane comes to mind. The number of such Trump inhibiting instances is too numerous to report here.

One conjecture I have not seen yet occurred to me as Trump's outrageous attacks on our democracy get exposed: I wonder who's behind the insane assassination of Iran's nuclear chief?

The main reported suspect is Israel, but denials have been issued which some have found questionable. The arguments favoring what was allegedly done by Israel appeared in a frightening cocksure editorial in the WSJ which you can read here.

The arrogance of power in the nuclear age should shock us into understanding how close to the triggering of such an unthinkable event which could be the use of a nuclear weapon to avenge this killing.

The history of how major wars start is full of instances of inadvertency! The assassination of Franz Ferdinand triggered WW One and we just saw in that PBS documentary Rise of the Nazis how WW Two with timely leadership intervention by German President Paul Von Hindenburg could have been avoided!

From the first use of such weapons by the U.S. to end WW Two the world has lived in fear of a repeat use of what could finish civilization as we know it on Earth.

Many nations have nukes, but it only takes one insane user perhaps abetted by another insane helper who would lend Iran a bomb to create disaster.

Living in DC exposes me to asking and receiving many opinions. One came from a veteran observer of international affairs including those of Iran, whose conjecture about the possible origin of the attack was aligned with mine.

He noted that,

> "I am not a politician, but common sense tells me the following:
>
> Killing Iranian Nuclear chief could be a political set-up, managed and planned by Trump and Netanyahu.

> And its real purpose could be to make more difficult the president-elect from resuming diplomacy with Tehran.
>
> And Iran will likely not make any stupid move now. They will wait for Biden's Administration to take over and talk again to solve their problems peacefully.
>
> This is my understanding. I could be wrong."

Of course one veteran observer strongly disagrees with the WSJ's editorial.

> "Mohsen Fakhrizadeh was slain Friday when a gunman ambushed him in his car near Tehran. Supreme Leader Ayatollah Ali Khamenei vowed revenge on Saturday, and pledged to continue the work of the man some called Iran's Oppenheimer.
>
> "This was a criminal act & highly reckless," tweeted Brennan, who ran the CIA under President Obama from 2013-2017. "It risks lethal retaliation & a new round of regional conflict. Iranian leaders would be wise to wait for the return of responsible American leadership on the global stage & to resist the urge to respond against perceived culprits."

> Iran's President Hassan Rouhani blamed Israel for the attack.
>
> Brennan said he didn't know whether a foreign government authorized or carried out the slaying, but said, "Such an act of state-sponsored terrorism would be a flagrant violation of international law & encourage more governments to carry out lethal attacks against foreign officials."

Former CIA Director Brennan's opinion backs up my concern over history as to how major wars accidentally start.

From 1945 until now we have lived knowing of the danger of a nuclear war.

And we know from daily media coverage that the insanity of powerful errant leadership is not extinct.

If indeed Pompeo's recent Israel visit with Netanyahu in any way encouraged this action at the start of Biden's term, we should know about it post haste!

When Biden is formally installed as President on January 20, 2020, he should get the facts and take steps to make Iran understand that this action will never characterize our behavior in his administration.

Look at the poised power of the members of the nuclear club of nations! If ever the UN had a role in pushing back the threat of such overreach it is now. Every powerful nation has a major stake in cooperation.

If a major nuclear war occurs would anyone be around to find out who instigated the assassination?

Of course, Biden needs to find out all the facts—which could come out even before his inauguration—and then speak decisively to separate his administration from any such future behavior.

Yes, Iran has violated its promises, but becoming a nuclear power is not becoming a nuclear attacker, an act which has not occurred since Hiroshima and Nagasaki.

Wonder if this conjecture will prove to be accurate, but if true it would be by far the most dangerous on the list of Trump's attacks on the Biden transition. Hope someone will do the investigation to see if this is correct.

# CHAPTER 24 THE REPUBLICAN PARTY, NOW THE TRUMP PARTY, HAS GONE VIRALLY DANGEROUS

*27 November 2020*

On Thanksgiving Day my wife and I spent in Fauci fashion just the two of us and felt we had much to be thankful for, but I guess for both of us the outcome of the Presidential election was high on our list of things to be thankful for.

In October I wrote an op ed entitled, "Rename the Republican Party?" which you can read in full here.

We couldn't know how Trump would behave when he lost by nearly 6 million votes, but his refusal to cede when the votes were counted and re-counted is historic misbehavior. The lying Trump continuing to argue for election fraud makes the Nixon coverup of the Watergate break in seem almost ineptly naïve.

The fact that for many years that party had lost its way is well documented by a 10/23/18 piece by Terry Gross of National Public Radio, entitled "Republican Voter Suppression Efforts Are Targeting Minorities".

You can read the entire piece here but its initial paragraphs spell out its misbehavior:

"Since the 2010 elections, 24 states have implemented new restrictions on voting. Alabama now requires a photo ID to cast a ballot. Other states such as Ohio and Georgia have enacted "use it or lose it" laws, which strike voters from registration rolls if they have not participated in an election within a prescribed period of time.

*Mother Jones* journalist Ari Berman, author of *Give Us the Ballot*, says that many of the restrictions are part of a broader Republican strategy to tighten access to the ballot — an effort that was bolstered in 2013 by the Supreme Court's Shelby County v. Holder ruling.

"[That] decision," Berman explains, "said that those states with the longest histories of discrimination no longer had to approve their voting changes with the federal government."

As a result, Berman says, "You're seeing a national effort by the Republican Party to try to restrict voting rights, and it's playing out in states all across the country."

Many of the new voting restrictions are occurring in states like Georgia, North Dakota and Kansas, which have critical

> races in the 2018 midterms. Berman says that it's still unclear what the impact of the restrictions will be on the upcoming elections, but he remains hopeful that the tide might be shifting on voter restrictions.
>
> Berman points out that an amendment to Florida's 2018 ballot would restore voting rights to more than 1 million former felons who are currently disenfranchised in the state."

My opinion about the main motivation of those 70 plus million Trump voters is fear. They are also anti-immigrant and clearly in favor of Trump's overt racism. Those are not pleasant facts, but they are obviously true. Naturally when these voters are confronted with those charges most of them will not admit such motivations, but such a block presents our democracy with serious problems for the future.

Question. How will Trump affect the Georgia senate races which will decide if Mitch McConnell keeps his job as Majority Leader?

A Thanksgiving Day 11/26 Washington Post article posits how keenly those Trump voters feel about the failure of their Republican officials to verify and support Trump on his untrue claims of voter fraud. You can read the piece here, but these paragraphs demonstrate the intensity.

"Sen. David Perdue was encouraging a crowd at a gun club south of Atlanta to support him and fellow Republican Kelly Loeffler in their bids for Georgia's Senate seats, which he called the only thing standing between America and "a radical socialist agenda."

But five minutes into the senator's speech, a man interrupted.

"What are you doing to help Donald Trump and this fraud case?" the man screamed, as one woman said "Amen" and the crowd applauded. "What are you doing to stop what's been going on here and this election fraud?"

The Republican candidates in Georgia's dual Senate runoff campaign are navigating a highly unusual political labyrinth — caught in the middle of an intraparty war that has erupted since President Trump narrowly lost the state to President-elect Joe Biden and has turned his fire on the Republican leadership there.

The infighting now threatens to turn off the very Republican voters Perdue and Loeffler need to stave off challenges from

> their Democratic rivals, Jon Ossoff and the Rev. Raphael Warnock.
>
> Trump and his allies have repeatedly, and falsely, accused Georgia Secretary of State Brad Raffensperger and Gov. Brian Kemp, both Republicans, of presiding over a fraudulent election. Trump has pushed the baseless claim that the Dominion Voting Systems machines used in Georgia were rigged as part of a global conspiracy, and Perdue and Loeffler have called for Raffensperger's resignation.
>
> But therein lies the conundrum: Perdue and Loeffler are traveling the state pleading with Republican voters to turn out on Jan. 5 — effectively asking Trump supporters to put their faith in the same voting system their president claims was manipulated to engineer his defeat."

The present top leaders of the party of Lincoln now frankly disgust me. What a tragedy. McConnell if remaining Majority Leader likely will little cooperate with Biden. And now with a packed Supreme Court we are going to see attacks on issues of vital importance be sidetracked or ignored as the deep divisions created by the lying and manipulation history of the Republican leadership has gained enough hegemony to delay progress at a very unpropitious time.

# CHAPTER 25 OVER HALF TRUMP'S VOTERS ARE CONVINCED OF ELECTION FRAUD

*23 November 2020*

One veteran editor and keen political observer responded to my November 20th op ed entitled "Trump undercuts American democracy" by emailing me this message: "I'm almost finished with Michael Cohen's book Disloyal at your recommendation. Fascinating insights into one of the most flawed humans ever to inhabit the planet."

My own brilliant editor added real impact to my 11/20 piece which opened with the Shutterstock photo of 3 young men wearing bright red tee shirts which carried the labels "In GOD We Trump".

I emailed my piece to many friends and associates and was pleased to get many replies which agreed with me. But I was more interested with the several I got which made clear that my views were very strongly disagreed with by the Trumpeters.

I am pleased to note that my views were echoed better than I had expressed them and in no uncertain terms by Mark Shields and David Brooks on Judy Woodruff's Friday, November 20th WETA evening news broadcast.

However, what scares me so much is that a majority of the 73 million who voted for Trump bought the Trump "Kool aid" and apparently agree or can't see what this neo-Nazi avalanche of lies is doing to our democracy.

A Presidential transition has never since George Washington been so handled by the incumbent.

The several negative responses I got from this last piece were truly frightening. Particularly this one from a wonderful masseuse my wife and I have used for years who was born and raised in Germany and who still goes there to visit her family.

Her message to me apparently didn't "get" Trump's lies at all. Here is her email to me:

> "November 21, 2020
>
> Dear Don,
>
> I am so disappointed that you support Biden and the socialist left. I always believed we were in agreement on the issue of immigration and lowering the world population and I always appreciated your wise words to that effect. I cannot believe that any normal person would vote for the senile and corrupt Biden.

> Trump is not perfect or even that likable but I like what he does for the country. He loves America and the American people.
>
> Trump traded his wealth in service to his country and Biden traded his country for his wealth. Not my own words but so very true.
>
> I am so sorry"

(Name withheld for her privacy's sake.)

In my muted and brief email reply I acknowledged our wide disagreements and suggested she watch the WETA series (PBS) entitled "Rise of the Nazis" but of course getting through to most of these folks is probably not possible.

Many doubtless have taken their news from hard right sources and likely don't read the mainstream daily papers and other media which Trump has spent 4 years calling "Fake Media". Finding truth in any of his pronouncements has been elusive, but the media has well documented his untruths so at least if one wants to know the facts, they are readily available.

I suspect few of his Kool Aid Kids have read Michael Cohen's book or Bob Woodward's Rage or Trump's niece, Mary Trump's book with its insider family analysis.

If they had, these bio exposures by such credible sources could have perhaps shed some small doubt on the validity of Rudi's preposterous ranting at his recent news conference. Sadly these claims of fraud persist despite the dangers so clearly expressed by Professor Timothy D. Snyder's history lesson article I cited in the Boston Globe.

Another astonishing email came from an MD who is a graduate of a top Eastern prep school and an Ivy League university. She and my daughter were classmates at both at about the same time (ages 60). This MD emailed me to stop sending her my "Ramblings" and asked me to acknowledge that I got her request. I of course immediately acknowledged her request without comment as any attempt there would likely be futile.

According to a recent poll by The Hill,

> "Roughly half of Republicans believe President Trump "rightfully won" the election, with 68 percent saying they had concerns about a "rigged" vote counting process in favor of President-elect Joe Biden, according to a new Reuters-Ipsos opinion poll released Wednesday.
>
> Overall, 73 percent of Americans polled in the Nov. 13-17 survey said they believed Biden won the election, while 5 percent say they thought Trump won.

> However, only 29 percent of Republicans believed that Biden had "rightfully won," compared to 52 percent of Republicans who said the same about Trump.
>
> The poll also reported that 55 percent of adults believed the 2020 election was "legitimate and accurate," a 7 percentage point decrease from a similar poll released following the 2016 election."

That Biden has his work cut out for him is not at question. And the majority of Trump's voters are not going to be convinced easily. However, Trump's refusal to concede or participate in the transition which will cause COVID deaths to increase may make his political future less powerful. And the lawsuits which will pursue him and his family when he departs The White House may cause him to have less time to spend on his golf courses. Over 400,000 COVID deaths are projected by March 1, 2021.

# CHAPTER 26 POST TRUMP? GRIDLOCK LOOMS FOR BIDEN

*20 November 2020*

Trump reprimanded a reporter at a recently rare news conference on Saturday, November 28 saying to the person I did not identify by name that "You don't speak to a President of the United States like that".

I don't know what the reporter said but I do know what my reaction was to his retort! Sorry I wasn't there to say, "If you behaved like you were President instead of lying and ranting about your recent thrashing at the polls, I wouldn't have had to ask the question which you answered like the dictator you hoped to become and now won't!"

Trump will, exactly as his niece Mary Trump predicted, continue to behave in ways unfortunately unfitting for the holder of our democracy's highest office, but then the standard for unethical behavior has been set by Senate Majority Leader Mitch McConnell.

In addition to not ceding his defeat, will he show at the inauguration? With the pandemic in progress, the traditional location may be different, and size of the crowd will doubtless be smaller than his pre-pandemic audience!

Unlike the incumbent, Senator McConnell has just been re-elected to his seat for 4 more years. Whether he retains his position as Majority Leader will shortly be determined by the 2 Senate runoff elections in Georgia in January. This is now considered likely to happen, but one never knows for sure.

Emotions are mixed about whether complete control of Congress by one party is good, but clearly if he retains his position McConnell's likely blocking of any major Biden legislative initiatives will result in gridlock.

I would think both sides will want to get together on an interim bill to provide benefits to the unemployed who now are suffering so badly.

Speaking of total control, the other tyranny McConnell engineered with the weak spined concurrence of his Republican colleagues was the packing of the Supreme Court, something FDR failed to do in the 1930's. I am sure Trump will add the fact that 3 new conservative Justices were confirmed on his watch was his major accomplishment.

So here we are, enmeshed in a vicious pandemic, with unemployment affecting many particularly small businesses while the stock market hits historic highs.

Of course, the lame duck incumbent quickly lauded the stock high as proof of his excellent handling of his job, as COVID deaths hit 265,000!

And of course, Trump claims great credit for the astonishing speed drug companies—many not U.S.

companies—accomplished in producing vaccines which now await final FDA scrutiny. Probably months will pass while the vaccines are distributed before we can all feel comfortable in resuming pre-COVID activities.

So, gridlock looms for Biden, and Georgia voters have a key decision to make on January 5th. Question: would you as a Georgia voter want Trump to come to campaign for the incumbent Republican senators?

Actually, as a Democrat, I guess I would hope he comes, even as he flies in on Air Force One at taxpayer expense to try to maintain Congressional gridlock and expand the wealth gap between rich and poor!

# CHAPTER 27 TRUMP UNDERCUTS AMERICAN DEMOCRACY

*20 November 2020*

Once years ago, I had the personal pleasure of dining with Norman Lear at his home in LA thanks to the recommendation of his able aide Virginia Carter. Only 6 of us and Norman and it was a delightful experience. What a creative genius and he is still alive at 98.

His multiple creations still resonate today, but especially for me his "All in the Family" series with Carroll O'Connor as Archie Bunker. That Norman is at 98 a proven feminist was evident as when he divorced his 2nd wife Frances, she got over $100 million. Ok, maybe community property law prevailed but still…

I was reminded of Archie Bunker's personal characteristics when on November 18th, Donald Trump's niece, Mary Trump was being interviewed by Don Lemon on his late-night CNN program.

Mary's 2020 insider tell all book, "Too Much and Never Enough: How My Family Created the World's Most Dangerous Man" proved to be a powerfully insightful and comprehensive exposé about President Trump's inner psyche.

It doubtless took courage by her in exposing herself to what must have been difficult attacks, not only from other Trumps and Donald's inner circle, but also likely from some of those 73 million presumably loyal Americans who voted for Donald Trump despite his well-publicized idiosyncrasies.

The continuing likely loyalty of too many of these 73 million who drank Trump's "Kool aid" propaganda stands starkly out as something that could exacerbate the future survival of our democracy. By continuing his manic behavior, Trump keeps trying to agitate and motivate these voters against the overwhelmingly effective democracy we enjoy.

Are these Trump supporting voters largely white uneducated rural Americans? I don't know. However, the ones I have seen screaming on TV saying Trump won the election or lost because of fraud seem to be mostly white males and females who are either conscious or unconscious of being racists, who continue to believe his lies about how he and they are being screwed by a corrupt system.

Democratic government is certainly not perfect, but as Winston Churchill commented in 1947 "Indeed it has been said that democracy is the worst form of government except for all those other forms that have been tried from time to time."

This failure to realize the fragility of democracy, Folks, eases the ability of aspiring dictators, who have used that formula throughout history to gain their anti-democratic goals. You recall Yale Professor Timothy D. Snyder's November 11, 2020 Boston Globe column which you can read again here. The article's opening title is worth repeating "Trump's Big Election Lie pushes America toward autocracy"; Clinging to power by claiming you are the victim of internal enemies is a very dangerous tactic; Don't underestimate where this can go."

A 2019 paperback book, "How Democracies Die" by Steven Levitsky is also well worth reading.

In short, as Trump's niece Mary Trump in effect told TV host Don Lemon in her interview on CNN on November 18th the President cares nothing about his supporters except as they will give him the necessary political clout after he leaves office to perhaps run again—the law permits 2 terms only so Obama or some attractive alternative candidate for example can't run again.

Meantime his niece is convinced Trump won't concede defeat or facilitate an orderly transition that since George Washington's time has historically until now occurred! Obama made Trump's accession as easy as possible in 2017. The outrage many feel at Trump's present behavior has not been replicated by most of his party members including Mitch McConnell.

Mary Trump is further convinced he cares nothing about the 250 thousand deaths from COVID.

It has been reported that his White House, where he hunkers down because, as Mary noted "losing" was the worst thing one could do as a Trump, he will be content to ignore any actions on the pandemic except to laud (and claim credit for) the vaccines which are coming but likely not widely available for months!

You could easily and gladly embrace and even laugh at all those characters on Lear's tv show All in the Family, but not at so many of those in the Trump family. Have Trump's supporters no shame or embarrassment? Let's see!

If his current behavior doesn't tip off his voters about his objective which is to gain great personal undemocratic power, our democratic future will be seriously affected by his ominous presence.

# CHAPTER 28 ARE WE NEEDLESSLY STUPIDLY POLITICALLY DIVIDED?

*16 November 2020*

A primary Republican mantra for the richest among us continues to feature the attack on any new taxes!

And that position evokes cheers as they and others who should know better envision the newly packed Supreme Court—which it may not—taking away Obama Care. Hopefully, that will not happen, but mindless ideologues can win and are too often these days prevailing as the rest of this op ed argues.

Sharing wealth as Bernie Sanders wants us to consider is not socialism! It is simply making sure the poor don't rebel against the wealth disparity in the world's wealthiest nation.

I'd call Bernie an Equitist!! As he often notes, we are the richest nation in the world, but that wealth is now badly balanced.

Not raising taxes is the mantra of the rich but what the growing number of our billionaires should be realizing is that not sharing a reasonable amount of that huge wealth is failing to buy an insurance policy against the anger represented by many of those 71 million votes for Trump, even as misunderstood as those voters apparently are in why they supported him.

Trump ironically was standing in the way of these voters. What they really wanted was more equity.

Trump succeeded early in his term by enacting his overdone corporate tax cuts for the richest among us!

Part of Trump's political cover story for his new constituents involved hypocritically feigning fealty for one religion whose leadership is awash in pedophilia and whose arrogant strictures against reproductive choice for women are designed to keep them from attaining their full range of occupational attainments. The stupidity of female denigrating, and lack of equality has certainly not subsided, but Senator Harris's election is a promising start.

The Catholic leadership's positions have of course also been greatly abetted by the evangelicals who say ditto to such outdated dangerous restrictions on liberty as for example represented by the enlightened Roe v Wade decision in 1973!

The answers of course are not prohibiting or inhibiting choice, but simply keeping religious choice out of secular law making.

The Roman Empire foundered on excess which our super rich could easily emulate but we can fervently hope will not. Why?

Well across the world in China we see that powerful dictatorship tightening its grip on allowing its citizens freedom by installing massive technological surveillance devices. And now we are horrified to observe its willful destruction of Hong Kong's superb free market example.

A positive future for us and the world would be our willingness to extend our wealth to all our citizens as insurance against the stupid embrace of maintaining the wealth gap that now divides us.

Bernie's equitism is not socialism and certainly wouldn't break us, but rather release us from the trap of failing to reduce the inequalities of health care, minimum wages, etc. that likely motivated many of those misguided 71 million.

Yes, small businesses could be exempted from minimum wage laws but surely not paying a living wage would attract those on less to keep seeking work with larger businesses which were subject to paying living wages.

# CHAPTER 29 TRUMP IS A DANGEROUS THREAT TO OUR DEMOCRACY

*13 November 2020*

The moral weakness shown by many leaders in the Republican Party over the past 4 years of the disastrous Trump Administration has been further revealed by Trump's current failure to acknowledge his defeat.

During "Rise of the Nazis" a PBS program on WETA on Tuesday evening, November 10th, I watched an eerie recital of how the political maneuvering by ambitious ruthless politicians who failed to understand Hitler's sinister aims led to disaster. At one point in his accession to Chancellor, Hitler claims he will "make Germany great again".

Trump got 72 million American votes and while Biden got 5 million more, Trump's party, for that is what the Republican Party has become, sees his future popularity as a highly useable ticket to power.

I suggest it will be important for us to read and heed an article by Timothy Snyder in the Boston Globe which appeared on November 11th entitled "Trump's Big Election Lie pushes America toward autocracy–Clinging to power by claiming you are the victim of internal enemies is a very dangerous tactic. Don't underestimate where this can go." You can read it in full here.

This article's first paragraphs are especially worthy of your attention:

> "When you lose, it is good and healthy to know why. In the First World War, the conflict that defined our modern world, the Germans lost because of the overwhelming force assembled by their enemies on the Western Front. After the Americans entered the war, German defeat was a matter of time. Yet German commanders found it convenient instead to speak of a "stab in the back" by leftists and Jews. This big lie was a problem for the new German democracy that was created after the war, since it suggested that the major political party, the Social Democrats, and a national minority, the Jews, were outside the national community. The lie was taken up by the Nazis, and it became a central element of their version of history after they took power. The blame was elsewhere.
>
> It is always tempting to blame defeat on others. Yet for a national leader to do so and to inject a big lie into the system puts democracy at great risk. Excluding others from the national community makes democracy impossible in principle and refusing to accept defeat makes it

impossible in practice. What we face now in the United States is a new, American incarnation of the old falsehood: that Donald Trump's defeat was not what it seems, that votes were stolen from him by internal enemies — by a left-wing party. "Where it mattered, they stole what they had to steal," he tweets. He claims that his votes were all "Legal Votes," as if by definition those for his opponent were not.

Underestimating Donald Trump is a mistake that people should not go on making. Laughing at him will not make him go away. If it did, he would have vanished decades ago. Nor will longstanding norms about how presidents behave make him go away. He is an actor and will stick to his lines: It was all a fraud, and he won "by a lot." He was never defeated, goes the story; he was a victim of a conspiracy. This stab-in-the-back myth could become a permanent feature of American politics, so long as Trump has a bullhorn, be it on Fox or on RT (formerly Russia Today) — or, though Democrats might find this unthinkable, as an unelected president remaining in power."

Think about how this plays out, Folks. Snyder is clear as he continues writing,

> "After all, a claim that an election was illegitimate is a claim to remaining in power. A coup is under way, and the number of participants is not shrinking but growing. Few leading Republicans have acknowledged that the race is over. Important ones, such as Mitch McConnell and Mike Pompeo, appear to be on the side of the coup. We might like to think that this is all some strategy to find the president an exit ramp. But perhaps that is wishful thinking. The transition office refuses to begin its work. The secretary of defense, who did not want the army attacking civilians, was fired. The Department of Justice, exceeding its traditional mandate, has authorized investigations of the vote count. The talk shows on Fox this week contradict the news released by Fox last week. Republican lawmakers find ever new verbal formulations that directly or indirectly support Trump's claims. The longer this goes on, the greater the danger to the Republic."

Have I got your attention? The rest of what Snyder says is equally chilling and relevant so please read it all and take heed.

Snyder concludes by saying, "This is no time to mince words. In the interest of the Republic and of their own party, Republicans should accept the results." Indeed!!!!!

# CHAPTER 30 BIDEN WINS! EMOTIONS? RELIEF, PRIDE, AND EMBARRASSMENT!

*9 November 2020*

Slightly after noon EST on November 7th the major TV networks called Pennsylvania with its 20 Electoral votes for Joe Biden giving him 273 Electoral votes and making him the prospective 46th U.S. President Elect and Senator Kamala Harris the potential first woman VP in U.S. history.

As the results of the election unfolded, we were all clearly transfixed by its closeness. Neither side of our divided nation could believe the other side would dare vote for the opposite candidate.

But I was of course somewhat consoled that our democracy is surely working with the largest number of votes ever cast for President in our history! Pride!

Lots of emotions have surfaced, but for me one major emotion was simply embarrassment that 70 million–over 40 percent of us–voted AGAIN for Donald Trump and to return such a totally unfit person for our highest office. Yes, I guess my first emotion has to be one of very deep relief and thankfulness!

My embarrassment is further magnified by the constant reports that in defeat this soon to be ex-President will continue to be the political leader of the once proud GOP! It has been reported that the GOP's main constituency now is white male non college graduates who feel that many powerful liberal Democrats, as Mark Shields noted on WETA, are instead of being the party of beer drinkers, now prefer chardonnay. The rural areas of America went for Trump, the cities for Biden.

The anomaly of his record apparently was ignored by his supporters. The list is too long to fit in any column, but despite the catalog of Trump's failings offered by Bob Woodward's "Rage" and Michael Cohen's "Disloyal: A Memoir", this frightening number of Americans gave this wannabe burgeoning neo-Nazi their vote. I recall that in my lifetime it only took Hitler about 4 years to turn the German democracy into one of the most depraved chapters in human history.

Certainly, in fairness, Trump's failure to manage the Coronavirus pandemic is not the only record of management failure by governments around the world. However, his dishonesty in telling us of its lethality, lying being the hallmark of his behavior, presaged his record of surrounding himself with his disreputable cronies and mountebanks.

So sad that the many able and reputable people who came to help him early in his term left and were thereafter continually attacked.

Then the "Fire Fauci!" cries from his final campaign stop symbolized perfectly his willingness to bend truth and ignore science.

FDR tried to pack the U.S. Supreme Court in the 1930's and failed! Trump succeeded!

That he has destroyed his party's reputation as a party that half the voters in the U.S. saw as an entity to be trusted suggests a new GOP needs to be reorganized since a strong two-party system has proven such a bulwark in keeping the vital balance of power from getting as out of balance as it is now.

Where were the voices of those GOP senators as Trump bullied and bludgeoned his callous egotistical way forward because of their silent concurrence?

Hopefully, Republican U.S. Senators Toomey and Romney will shortly be joined by many others in expressing concern if not utter distain for the pathetic whining from this incumbent as he exits. Hope his exit will be better than I am guessing it will be.

These past months have elicited in all Americans a series of intense emotions.

Having been sequestered at home and very cautious when venturing out, my family and I (with one exception, my wife's brother) have to date not gotten Coronavirus but we all remain on high alert waiting for a vaccine which could be months away.

We thus have all felt anger, fear, frustration and yet gratitude for the luck we have had as we have avoided COVID-19.

Now the election judged by many of us as the most important in our lifetime is over.

With potentially 300 plus Electoral votes for Biden, Trump's threatened lawsuits are not likely to prove effective or even fundable! Trump's Atlantic City junk bond creditors offer perfect past examples of his willingness to lead the unwary down dead-end paths!

Biden has won but he will face a hostile Senate and a smaller House majority.

So, what emotions strike me now? Again, let me repeat: Embarrassment, pride that the system worked, and great relief but also some fear that the influence of Trump will continue to infect our body politic in ways which reduce our freedom and comity as a great nation!

# CHAPTER 31 THE CERTAINTY: MORE FUTURE FAILURES UNDER TRUMP IF RE-ELECTED

*21 October 2020*

I am totally uneasy as we approach 11/3 as the crazies, including sadly members of my own family, do not get the fact that Trump is so obviously a burgeoning neo-Nazi whose re-election could further damage our democracy beyond easy or even any acceptable repair.

We have lost much of our vaunted credibility as an international leader only to become a laughingstock for Putin, Chi and Kim.

Did you see this week on TV the massive military parade Chi hosted in China? He is flaunting his power. If Chi decides to take Taiwan which he may, can our recourse be a military defense? Such action could lead to a war neither of us could stop. More on that in a moment.

Remember with nostalgia what Kennedy was able to negotiate with Nikita Khrushchev in withdrawing Russian missiles from Cuba. Think about it. The so-called Monroe Doctrine for South America is dead, and the world of so-called big nation protected spaces is no longer without major war risk.

Our sad domestic situation has been made so traumatized by Trump's lies and the incursions of false stories from our major enemies be they Chi or Putin. Putin has Trump in his pocket.

Yes, as Tom Friedman recently noted, this our election becomes a pivotal moment on our history.

Our domestic political atmosphere has been so traumatized by Trump's lies and the incursions of false stories into our mass media from our major enemies that our election becomes a pivotal moment on our history.

There is of course still a reasonable chance that Biden will win, and his actions if he does will be seminal for our future.

Our record of stupid wars since Vietnam, where I lead a tour of experts to study a method of family planning in 1994 underlines for me that dismal record. Those poor yet wonderful people beat us and as a result should have taught us a lesson, but subsequently our international arrogance has continued. Yes, it can be argued that we saved South Korea from Kim's father, but we were joined in our military action with approval from the UN Security Council (its Russia representative was not there when the vote was taken).

Even after South Korea, our military-industrial complex and acquiescent Congress and Presidents were willing, to me it seems for perceived economic benefits for our domestic economy, to be stupid with "police actions" never obtaining Congressional approval, which was last obtained by FDR after Pearl Harbor. As some wise historians have already let us know, those police actions were futile, dangerous, and needlessly expensive, as well as corruptive of our moral standards for international behavior.

We must understand that wars of any kind now could start a nuclear war which will make our planet so much less livable that the survivors might not be glad they survived.

So here we are divided by false news into hate postures which have put the two sides at each other's throats and made this election the most important of my lifetime. At nearly 90 I can only grieve at the legacy of foolishness my generation is handing on to the next.

Biden, if elected, actually has a shot at fixing our bedeviled republic. He has nothing to lose and could take actions so important to overcoming the dangerous legacy of hate and dissolution which Trump has generated.

Our economy, which by the way was in no way greatly improved by Trump or prior Presidencies, but rather as the result of our basic freedoms to create new businesses and opportunities for us citizens, and which could continue to do so under a calm, moderate and cooperative Congress and Chief Executive. Even the blatant packing by Trump and the Republican Party of the Supreme Court could prove to be manageable because even errant new Justices will likely see the damage to cutting off health care for the poorest and going against the Stare Decisis precedence of Roe vs Wade and Casey after 47 years of successful experience.

Think carefully, Trumpers, as while you likely have already voted you will regret deeply your choice. Now you are listening to his raging rants at the unprotected faces of his rally fans from this potential neo-Nazi incumbent. You perhaps subsequently will realize if he is re-elected how, he unmercifully adopted these stances to enable his ego maniacal personality to entice your worst instincts, just as he was able to the sell the illusion of gain to Michael Cohen, his 12 yearlong insider lawyer-fixer, who gave up everything for Trump's song of power–which was unconscionable power for him and also not you.

# CHAPTER 32 HOW TRUMP BECAME PRESIDENT? READ "DISLOYAL: A MEMOIR"!

*14 October 2020*

When I noticed that the disgraced and convicted Trump lawyer Michael Cohen's book "Disloyal: A Memoir" had made the top ten list of non-fiction books in The NY Times Book Review section I was motivated to go to Amazon to read his book's reviews.

Those reviews were mostly given 4 or 5 stars but didn't seem to say specifically why. Although some said the book was a page turner they couldn't put down.

So, I bought the book and am so glad I did. Yes, Folks, it is a page turner!

Cohen tells a fascinating story. Already a wealthy and successful lawyer with a lovely wife and two attractive children a boy and a girl, he did some routine legal work for Donald Trump Jr and then met Trump Sr for whom he solved a nasty problem which began a fascinating tale of his being seduced into being a full-time employee who agreed to do all the dishonest tasks Trump needed fixed.

At this point one must ask how credible is his narrative?

To me the detail Cohen offers based on his 12 year access to Trump's perfidious doings seems very credible.

Reading for me, during this pandemic, has become a fixture of life as I seek to keep my mind engaged in this unique time, while staying safe at home.

So amidst this plethora of news options, one gets quite good at judging the bogus from the true or the cynical from the naive.

Thus, as mentioned before, when I saw Michael Cohen's exposé book listed as one of the top ten non-fiction books on the October 11, 2020, The NY Times Book Review section list I went to Amazon and started reading the reviews.

Turns out, this disgraced Trump fixer is a compelling writer. His story rings frighteningly true and offers voters insights about Trump which are more devastating than any I have read so far.

Cohen's details are so meticulously presented that his claimed sincere regret at being an intimate player in this felonious world he worked in seems totally plausible.

Clearly, he got caught which prompted his outcry, but the story he tells is still riveting.

He spares himself no excuses for his illegal and morally reprehensible behavior and fully admits his culpability.

That his employer seems better defined by these disclosures serves a useful purpose as voting in what will be a crucial election gets underway.

Cohen became disenchanted with Trump by 2014 but urged Trump to run for President which he grandly did on June 16$^{th}$ as he descended the Trump Tower staircase; start reading on page 207 for the campaign story.

Trump's love for Putin gets expressed beginning on page 245. Read Cohen's claimed implications on page 250.

Cohen's downfall after Trump is President defies understanding but Trump abandons him without so acknowledging and Cohen is tried, convicted, and sentenced to 36 months in Federal prison for white collar criminals at Otisville NY in the Catskills.

Cohen's subsequent treatment offers frightening examples of how power can corrupt Constitutional rights.

Cohen's behavior for Trump was heinous. His fate fails to elicit my sympathy but every American should read this story so they can decide how they feel.

Bob Woodward's best-selling book "Rage" was number one on the Times non-fiction list on October 11$^{th}$. I just read the book and to me it gives greater credibility to the claims detailed meticulously by Cohen!

I'm going to carefully keep my copy as I suspect this first edition from this little-known publisher will become increasingly valuable.

# CHAPTER 33 TRUMP IS DESPERATE, BUT DON'T GET TOO CONFIDENT

*11 October 2020*

That Trump is showing signs of desperation even as his dangerous egotism springs forth at every public occasion he stages, even at the risk of infecting anyone in his orbit at the White House or elsewhere. We can't know now, but it is likely that quite a few prior Trump supporters are now listening to the rantings of the incumbent and changing their minds.

This is an example of the Trump email I get several times daily:

> "Friend,
>
> I left Walter Reed after receiving incredible care and I'm feeling really good! In fact, I feel better than I did 20 years ago.
>
> I'm telling you: **Don't be afraid of Covid. Don't let it dominate your life! This is the greatest country in the world, and under the Trump Administration, we have developed some really great drugs and knowledge. WE WILL BEAT THIS, TOGETHER!**

> The love and support from Americans from all over the world has been incredible and is something I'll never forget. When I saw many great Patriots outside of the hospital supporting me, I knew I had to drive by and thank them!
>
> Now, I am fired up and ready to **KEEP FIGHTING FOR YOU! This is the FINAL STRETCH of the Election and we can't take any days off.**
>
> We have come a long way these past three and a half years, but we're not done yet. Important steps need to be taken if we're going to **Make America Great Again,** and the only way to do it is if we <u>WIN FOUR MORE YEARS.</u>
>
> I know you want to secure another VICTORY just as much as I do, which is why I'm prepared to do something HUGE."

This simply warns us about what happened in 2016 where Hillary Clinton was a shoo-in and then was not.

We can't know how many Trump supporters might defect and if these numbers might impact key battleground states. Guessing by the experts is rampant.

I was heartened by Judy Woodruff's WETA interview with Mark Shields and David Brooks on October 9th but even they are still cautious, although quite optimistic.

Witness the powerful big business community gaining control of our government and transferring our historically high National Debt to us taxpayers. They fail to pay taxes to maintain our government services—look at our postal mess and our failing underfunded agencies. Any mention of paying their fair share of taxes gets manic disapproval from big business while the little businesses and the rest of us get screwed year after year.

I encourage you to reread my September 14, 2020 OP ED about how that happened here: it is entitled, "How U.S. Taxpayers Assumed the National Debt of the Super Rich."

Research over the long run shows that higher taxes—even over 50%—haven't ruined incentive or capital growth. Biden says if he is elected no one earning less than $400,000 a year will get a tax increase.

The richest woman in the world is the divorced wife of Jeff Bezos who is worth over $50 billion. Billionaires are commonplace in America today.

So, we can presume from the rising stock market that sophisticated market watchers know that a Biden victory would not be bringing in SOCIALISM as Trump argues.

Heavens, if one looks at even the amount of government spending on basic research, services, and health for us all, it was not enough! More could have been spent and the 40 year Republican record of cutting taxes on the wealthy has left an unconscionable number of our poorer citizens unserved in basic ways.

That only one more Presidential debate will take place seems a favorable development and if Trump behaves as he did before in the October 22nd debate that should not change the favorable scenario Brooks and Shields offered Friday evening on WETA.

Stay alert and stay very safe if you can as the wide distribution of the vaccine is months away.

# CHAPTER 34 HOW U.S. TAXPAYERS ASSUMED THE NATIONAL DEBT OF THE SUPER RICH

*14 September 2020*

The NY Times Magazine has a special section in its Sunday September 13 issue entitled "Greed is good except when it is bad" about the landmark essay by Milton Friedman it published on September 13, 1970, in which he said the social responsibility of business is to increase its profits.

You can start your reading of this supplement here.

In this special new section 50 years later, the Times assembled many corporate leaders and many prestigious economists including an early and severe critic of Friedman's thesis.

One quoted was also like Friedman a Nobel Prize winner in Economics (his in 2001), Columbia Professor Joseph Stiglitz who in his statement for this supplement says:

> "The absurdity of his [Friedman's] analysis is seen most clearly by an example. Assume, in our imperfect democracy, that coal-mining companies use campaign contributions to block laws restricting pollution. Assume you're a manager of one of the host of other companies

> that could spend a little bit of money to reduce pollution. You care about your children, your family, your community, but also about your business. Would you be irresponsible, as Friedman suggests, to curb your company's pollution, because in doing so you reduce its profits? Would it be irresponsible for you to persuade others in your industry to do the same, even if you weren't able to persuade Congress to pass a bill to compel you to do so? I think not. If you and others like you acted in this manner, societal welfare would be increased.
>
> Friedman's position is based on a misconception of both economics and the Democratic political process. Yes, in an ideal world,"

But then we aren't in such a world—we agree.

Much more of this anniversary supplement in the NY Times Magazine allows credit for the mistaken promotion of Friedman's theory goes to the libertarians which is doubtless useful to acknowledge. The Kochs for example.

You can start reading about the libertarians here.

I read the remarks of all the others in this Times supplement, many agreeing with Stiglitz. So do I.

But let's let all the opinions expressed by the "I knew it all along how wrong Milton was" commentators in this supplement have their day IF only someone would care to comment on the article which I wrote on this web site.

I knew Milton and Rose and had occasion to meet and talk with them on many occasions, as they were neighbors of mine when I lived in San Francisco. I bought his "Kool aid" along with so many others.

But now is a great time for the truth about the net effect of this Friedman greed plan.

What I opined in my recent op ed is that the failure over 40 years to raise taxes to meet the rising costs of human welfare provided by the governments of America—so business could pay its fair share as we went along—at every level has gradually transferred our huge national debt to the taxpayers of America while corporations using ways to cut taxes have produced profits which they used to buy their own stock, pay outlandish wages and benefits to their top executives and make more billionaires than ever before in America!

Biden, if elected, has promised to raise corporate taxes to 28 percent from 21 now, but proven historical economic studies show that the incentive for making innovation is not stunted by taxes at far higher levels such as 48 percent or even more!

The incumbent has added 3 trillion to our bloated National Debt and the 28 percent will be inadequate to avoid adding more debt should Biden win.

The snookered 40 percenters who cheer madly to MAGA are just asking for more economic slavery.

I seek only the small favor. We could start acknowledging the truth that my friend Milton's greed plan was what lead to the transfer of our National Debt to us taxpayers.

And admitting that more needs to be done by the famous rich and the legislatures they control to fix the problem than simply now stating their agreement Milton was wrong.

C'mon your experts, fess up to the fact that more taxes are urgently needed to help our burgeoning social and environmental problems. 28 percent is a start but not enough. That's not socialism, it is just fairness and common sense to correct our failure to restrain crony capitalism which has made the gap between rich and poor in America so wide.

I can only hope the simple admission by these worthy experts of how we taxpayers assumed our National Debt will be made by some of these big companies and the economic theorists who wrote for this timely NY Times Magazine supplement on Milton's 50th anniversary.

# CHAPTER 35 TRUMP'S BEHAVIORAL QUALITIES BRING FIERCE OPPOSITION FROM MANY IN BOTH PARTIES

*11 September 2020*

We now have exactly 53 days beginning on September 11th until Election Day, but the matter of the preference of either candidate about many policy issues has become muted by the morality issue.

Furthermore, one can argue whether or not the incumbent should take one course or another, but the matter of his competence in handling the Coronavirus pandemic is now no longer a question.

Perhaps it was the publication of Bob Woodard's book "Rage" which seemed to many including me to be the final straw but the piling up of negative opinion from both political sides has been simply overwhelming.

We all recall Woodward's influence on Nixon's exit, but now he defends himself for not revealing Trump's January and February knowledge of the danger of Coronavirus by saying in the Associated Press 9/10 piece entitled "Woodward defends decision to withhold Trump's virus comments" which its author Hillel Italie says that Woodward,

> "facing widespread criticism for only now revealing President Donald Trump's early concerns about the severity of the coronavirus, told The Associated Press on Wednesday that he needed time to be sure that Trump's private comments from February were accurate.
>
> In Woodward's upcoming book on Trump, "Rage," the president is quoted saying the virus was highly contagious and "deadly stuff" at a time he was publicly dismissing it as no worse than the flu. Woodward, the celebrated Washington Post journalist and best-selling author, spoke with Trump more than a dozen times for his book.
>
> "He tells me this, and I'm thinking, 'Wow, that's interesting, but is it true?' Trump says things that don't check out, right?" Woodward told the AP during a telephone interview. Using a famous phrase from the Watergate era, when Woodward's reporting for the Post helped lead to President Richard Nixon's resignation, Woodward said his mission was to determine, "What did he know and when did he know it?""

You can read the entire article here.

Even the Wall Street Journal now must realize editorially that it is looking foolish to continue unabated its Trump stump. Hence this piece on its Opinion Page.

I refer you to the 9/10 editorial page column by Walter Olsen entitled "Never Trump, Now More Than Ever" who notes "When the crisis came as a pandemic, a different president, conscious of his limitations, might have stepped back to let Anthony Fauci and Deborah Birx do the talking. But Mr. Trump has bluffed his way through life claiming to know more than the experts. He needs to be the groom at every wedding and the infant at every christening."

Olsen closes by saying,

> "Remember the "character counts" conservatives? The classicists who went back beyond the Federalist Papers to the Greeks and Romans to ground conservatism in civitas and virtue? Who thought deeply about the dangers to the republic from a man on horseback, a demagogic flatterer of the people, who preaches "I alone can fix it"?
>
> "But he fights." He is a litigious man who has openly boasted of using losing lawsuits to harm his critics. Yes, a president needs some combative spirit, but it should be discerning—especially when aimed at fellow Americans—and give way in due season to a spirit of reconciliation.

> We don't know when the next crisis will come. It might be a close election in which Mr. Trump needs to accept the decision of the judiciary. We might need national unity. Instead, this man's tweets are the ground glass in the national milkshake.
>
> A high degree of social trust is needed both for a dynamic economy and for the rule of law. But as legal scholar Orin Kerr puts it, "the president's signature move is to attack the legitimacy of everyone and every institution who is not in lockstep with him."
>
> Some offer the "Flight 93 election" theory, in which every four years we face a last-chance, bet-the-country abyss. I don't buy it. Our country has a system of rotation in office. The other party gets its turn, and the country survives. It will survive Donald Trump, too. But the country should not have to face four more years of him."

Yes, 53 days during which time we will have the famous debates which were so crucial in 1960 when Kennedy beat Nixon. But neither of these men then were the incumbent who has to speak for his lying behavior or his multiple other moral failings.

So, we need a new shuffle of the deck, and while Biden is not highly touted by many, he represents a return to proven competence and certainly a higher moral standing.

# CHAPTER 36 THE RICH GOT TO CHARGE OUR RECORD NATIONAL DEBT TO US TAXPAYERS

*5 September 2020*

Far smarter people than me have now figured out what happened to our bloated national debt, but apparently were loath to tell us until the deal was done.

Certainly, the joyous tax cuts for the wealthy from the high 30's to 21 percent for corporations done by Trump in 2017 accelerated the situation, but clearly the tax increase myth that by raising taxes we would cut innovation and would cut productivity is simply not true!

Fostered by Milton Friedman and the University of Chicago school economists that got adopted as gospel by the Reagan Administration in 1980 has not helped the average citizen but has built a rich autocracy which now governs Congress and has driven many of our poorer citizens to the wall.

In short, the rich got to charge our bloated national debt to us taxpayers.

The September 3, 2020, front page Wall Street Journal story tells the story, but for me the article doesn't articulate clearly enough what I just wrote in the previous sentence.

You can read the entire page one WSJ article here.

You have read a lot about the billionaires from Tim Cook, Jeff Bezos, Elon Musk or the benign guru from Omaha, Warren Buffett, and his brilliant and publicly focused friend Bill Gates, Jr, but perhaps you don't know that MacKenzie Scott has become the world's richest woman. MacKenzie Scott — philanthropist, author, and ex-wife of Amazon CEO Jeff Bezos — is now the wealthiest woman in the world. Read about her here in CNN Business.

Never in American history have the billionaires been so numerous but the philanthropy of many such as Buffett and Gates should not and cannot be the substitute for effectively functioning taxpayer governmental agencies.

Like all the oligarchies of history that get so out of balance, this one will not work in the best interests of our democracy.

Tim Cook just sold some of his Apple stock which netted him a huge low taxed capital gain. That money will be used but where? Too much is too much. You can read about that here.

Henry Ford, not lauded for many of his racial attitudes, did understand that to sell his model A and T cars early in the last century one needed to give workers enough wages to buy them, and he paid his workers a high daily wage to make that happen.

Many others business and governmental leaders also realized that fact through the post-World War II and Korean War years, as we embarked on a number of foolish foreign wars to test our bloated military establishment's arms, which has given us much well-paid domestic employment and huge profits to those defense companies.

Too bad that as we spend annually over $700 billion for defense but find that the U.S. Post Office of $7 billion yearly and loses over $8 billion is considered worthy by some of being made a political football instead of confirming its key tradition as a major employer of middle-class citizens.

You can read about our defense budget here.

You can read about the Post Office here.

Yet we must give Reagan and Mikhail Gorbachev huge credit for making nuclear war less likely.

But the ultimate view of Friedman, that corporations should only be focused on profit, was the view that got us to where we are today. Supply side economics always fails and for 40 years we have been going in the wrong direction.

Trump's reelection would truly continue us on that wrong road to economic and social disaster.

His charge of Biden being a socialist is thus, based on the record, so far from reality that compared to what 40 years of oligarchy capitalism has created, we can only assume he seeks to finalize the dictatorship of oligarchy capitalism in his reelection.

Yet his snookered 40 percent base apparently don't or won't wake up.

So Trump's 2nd term fear agenda is based on waving American flags, pushing the Christian religion as primary to all Americans, being for the 2nd Amendment so non-governmental gun bearers can go to politically Democratic cities to "help" police put down peaceful protesters, being against safe abortions for women, and saying after Charlottesville that racists are okay, seems to have not penetrated the consciousness of that 40 percent who kowtow to his view as the best way forward.

Can't wait for the 3 debates between Biden and Trump to see how the incumbent handles answers to the above circumstances.

# CHAPTER 37 TRUMP/BIDEN: ONLY 61 DAYS TO GO

*3 September 2020*

Even before post-convention campaigns began you doubtless had long tired of the barrage of fundraising emails from the candidates.

I am now still getting at least 5 or 6 a day from both Trump and/or his proxies and Biden and/or his proxies. Few people now even open them I suspect.

I did open this one today from Trump which begins,

> "Did you hear the news, Friend?
>
> I just announced how I'm going to keep FIGHTING FOR YOU with my second-term agenda.
>
> From the day I became your President, I have put America First with every decision that I make. Unfortunately, the Democrats are threatening to DESTROY everything if they TAKE BACK the Nation.
>
> We cannot let that happen, Friend. Where the Left sees American darkness, I see American greatness.

> These next few weeks will be absolutely brutal as we get closer to Election Day. I need my BEST supporters to step up to the front lines and help me WIN BIG so that I can implement my critical second-term agenda."

Then the spot takes one to the pitch for money. There's plenty of money on both sides already, but this election could be very close.

Trump in 2016 greatly used the immigration issue to get elected by making many voters fear a foreign invasion.

So far Trump's 2nd term agenda has featured his replaying the fear card while much of our citizens are suffering the effects of the pandemic and economic distress, except for the super or the near rich whose wealth gap has been developing for 40 years ever since Milton Friedman's claim that profits should be the sole goal of business was adopted as orthodoxy under Reagan.

Electing a President means bringing in a cast of characters to serve him. For an incumbent, we know who those folks are or who they were if they are no longer there.

In Trump's case the in and out list is staggering even long before the present turmoil. Here the list as of October 2019 which you can read here courtesy of CNN Politics.

Serving and leaving gave those who served the chance to write a book which as in John Bolton's case was a best seller.

Regardless, the outcome in November is likely going to be very close and the Electoral College votes in a few states could swing the result. The headline in this 9/2/20 Washington Post article entitled, "How turnout and swing voters could get Trump or Biden to 270".

Bring the article up and play the various options. I did and found the way you can manipulate the numbers online most confirming of the potential narrowness of the margin to victory.

Some say the upcoming Presidential debates will be a key factor as they were with Nixon and Kennedy in 1960. Some think that the Postmaster Louis Dejoy has crippled the mail service so the vote-by-mail ballots will not get handled properly. Both sides agree that the result will be decided by the ardor of the contending voters.

The erratic behavior of the incumbent between now and in the 61 days until November 3 could ultimately cause some of his base to defect.

For example, the effect of the fact that Trump went to Kenosha despite the mayor and the Lt Governor asking him not to come is now unknown.

A friend just forwarded to me the August 30 speech of the Portland mayor Ted Wheeler who has been trying to defuse violence in his city for several months.

> "Last night's violence began with hundreds of supporters of Donald Trump

rallying and then driving into downtown Portland. They were energized and supported by the president himself.

President Trump, for four years we have had to live with you and your racist comments about Black people. We learned early about your sexist attitudes towards women. We have had to endure clips of you mocking a disabled man, we have heard your anti-democratic attacks on journalists. We have read your tweets slamming private citizens to the point of receiving death threats, and we've heard your direct attacks on immigrants including labeling Mexicans as murderers and rapists. We've heard you say that John McCain was not a hero because he was a prisoner of war and now you're attacking democratic mayors in the very institutions of democracy that have served our nation well since its founding.

Do you seriously wonder, Mr. President, why this is the first time in decades that America has seen this level of violence? It's you who have created hate in the division that has led to violence, Mr. President.

It's you who have not found a way to say the names of Black people killed by police officers, even as people in law-enforcement have and it's you who claimed the white supremacists are good people.

Your campaign of fear is as anti-democratic as anything you've done to create hate and vitriol in our beautiful country. You've tried to divide us more than any other figure in modern history and now you want me to stop the violence that you helped create.

What America needs is for you to be stopped so that we can come back together as one America while recognizing that we must demand that all people, black, brown, white, every color from every political persuasion pull together all people accountable in stopping racism and violence and we together are peaceful again under a new leadership that reflects who we really are, the people of this great nation.

President Trump you bring no peace, you bring no respect to our democracy. You, Mr. President, need to do your job as the leader of this nation and I, Mr. President, will do my job as the mayor of this city and we will both be held accountable as we should."

Yes, only 61 more days of this. Lots can happen either way.

# CHAPTER 38 TRUMP ELECTION RACISM QUESTIONS

*2 September 2020*

After watching Trump break any ethical standard to win re-election with a Bible in the air and a comment that George Floyd must be looking down from heaven with satisfaction at what his death has done to put down racism, I can only wonder at what the reaction of his core supporters will be. My guess is continued obeisance along with the Senate Republicans.

Of course, one could postulate that his promised veto of any effort to change the names of the U.S. Army bases named for Confederate Civil War generals is proof of his abject cynicism about racism. In so stating, I suspect his base would (violently?) disagree!

On June 11 and 12 our PBS station WETA in DC aired two 3 hour segments featuring Harvard Professor Henry Louis Gates Jr's films and books on Reconstruction (1864-1875) and the successful efforts thereafter by white Southerners who viciously and murderously took away from blacks the civil rights granted by the 13th, 14th and 15th Amendments to the U.S. Constitution which has allowed blacks a time of freedom and progress during the brief Reconstruction period.

Knowing about the history now has great bearing on whether or not the George Floyd murder will lead to real reform not just of policing but of correcting the huge imbalances of civil rights still suffered by black Americans.

This web site has been correctly incisive about the long-time success of religions to dictate unwise political influence over secular governments worldwide and certainly here in the US. Attacks on women's reproductive rights offers a prime example.

However as white racism flourished after Reconstruction in the South, black churches proved critical refuges for blacks beset by the KKK's violence and lynchings.

The disparity of opportunities for blacks exists to this day and makes the Floyd murder a significant chance for improving race relations but clearly not if we give The Great Divider Trump a second term.

In the 1930's I grew up in a small city near Pittsburgh. Pittsburgh spawned the Pittsburgh Courier a black paper of national reputation.

So many black musicians populated the national scene then whose work still stands as exemplary. I can still sing the lyrics along with Fats Waller as he plays Honeysuckle Rose, Ain't Misbehavin, or Hold Tight! With Lena Horne and Satchmo—Louie Armstrong—and Nat King Cole and countless others from whom we all got huge enjoyment. It is lamentable that despite these brilliant stars that blacks were still kept down by phony racial theories, lack of broad educational chances (there was one black male in my 1949 freshman class at Yale) and our dreadful history of slavery and its still present hangover today.

Did I after graduation personally engage in any public action to change that obvious condition? Nothing but my unbiased personal behavior in all my numerous contacts with African Americans. Too many of us white people pretended progress was being made. My marriage in middle life to a Jewish woman did not really educate me much about my racial ignorance.

Pittsburgh product August Wilson left his black Hill District for Minneapolis where he wrote his famous Hill District plays about the lives of blacks there. Again, eye opening but not sufficiently life changing for black Americans.

So back to now. Is voting for Trump the equivalent of voting for American version of Putin, Chi and Kim?? 40 percent of us won't see it that way.

A 2nd Trump term means further packing of the U.S. Supreme Court. It could be argued that not only our future but to a plausible extent the future of democratic governance here and elsewhere hangs on his being turned out of office!

Biden may not be everyone's idea of a dream candidate, but he is an intrinsically honorable person, highly qualified by his history to uphold our laws and encourage unity now so broken by Trump's relentless campaign of divisiveness.

# CHAPTER 39 TRUMP KEEPS THE RICH IN CHARGE

*28 August 2020*

What was the real message from the just concluded Republican National Convention? Was it to spread fear and keep most of America living paycheck to paycheck?

That should have been to many the main message from this week of the Republican National Convention which closed with Trump's final hate speech at the White House on August 27$^{th}$.

Sadly, widespread comprehension of what has happened to Americans since 1980 has not been understood, certainly not by the paycheck-to-paycheck Americans who are a key part of Trump's 40 percent base.

Meanwhile the U.S. stock market continues its upward surge which creates the erroneously false picture that we all are better off rather than the true picture that most of Americans are living paycheck to paycheck.

The Trump Administration has no plan except to keep those eager slaves in place for the rich since the rich now control our Congress and American politics in general. And most pundits on the left or right agree that Trump controls the Republican Party.

Fiscal restraint that used to be a Republican virtue has now become lost. But why not since now the wealthy control it all as we uncomfortably witness Trump's unprecedented and unethical use of "the people's house" for his acceptance speech to a tightly packed partisan audience who were largely unmasked in obedience to the examples set from on high! Wonder if any of those partisans will contract Covid-19.

This present situation of the huge gap between net worth and income of the rich and the rest of us was powerfully articulated in a new book by Kurt Andersen entitled "Evil Geniuses" which was the page one review in the August 23rd in the NY Times Sunday Book Review section. Andersen was also interviewed by Walter Isaacson on Amanpour.

You can see both here.

The great monopolistic Trusts which TR Roosevelt attacked in his time as President—you know, the Standard Oils and the railroad monopolies—are now replaced by the tech stock monopolies of Facebook, Google, Apple, and Amazon, who keep buying back stock with profits from the huge tax cut for the rich which Trump engineered.

Andersen tells us it started in the 1970's with Milton Friedman's claim that supply side economics would benefit us all. Sorry that my longtime neighbor in SF was so wrong.

By the way, Democrats were guilty of concurrence. In Andersen's book in Chapter 23 entitled "Winners and Losers in the Class War" we learn that Freidman's

> "supply-side premise—that tax rates at some very high level tend to persuade people to work less—is true."
>
> "Yet as Krugman says, 'the optimal tax rate on people with very high incomes is the rate that raises the maximum possible revenue.'" However, "Economic research shows convincingly that the self-defeating level of taxation is much higher than of highest federal income tax rate has been for the last forty years—apparently the disincentive effect doesn't kick in until you get up to a top marginal rate of at least 48 percent and maybe not until 76 percent or higher."

So now let's look at the tax rate situation. The highest personal tax rate for individuals is 37% if they have an income of $518,400 and file separately.

When Trump took office in 2017, the corporate tax rate was 35%, far below the heavier burdens of 48 or 78 percent, which research shows were not going to reduce work incentives to top earners.

Not good enough. Trump got approval to cut the corporate rate in 2017 to 21% which meant that the corporate tax rate raised $230.2 billion in 2019, accounting for 6.6% of federal revenue down from 9 percent in 2017.

No wonder companies have the money to buy back their stock or the rich keep getting richer, and the gap is going to get bigger and bigger.

This outrageous trend is at the heart of America's problems and only a sharp change in attitude will address it.

> "Meanwhile, in real life since 1980, the supply side low-tax-pay-itself magic has repeatedly failed to do the trick: the federal government is negligibly smaller, but the federal debt has more than tripled in real terms" (page 287).

Profit, as Milton Freidman claimed, is all good, and in 1980 Ronald Regan started with Democrat concurrence on the decades long march to the present big gap between the rich and the paycheck-to-paycheck Americans, many of whom were seen at this latest Republican National Convention cheering for more slavery!

New stocks in technology happily surface all the time. We can all be pleased with this wealth of new useful technology. However, although Salesforce, a new tech giant, which had record sales and ironically replaced Exxon (whose origins were John D. Rockefeller the First's giant oil monopoly) as one of the Dow Jones Industrial Average's top 30 stocks is letting workers go. Read it here.

So, MAGA means longer term wage slavery courtesy of the incumbent and his ilk who, with 4 more years, can tighten the noose so we will have more, not less, paycheck-to-paycheck workers!

Will the knowledge of this economic tyranny seep into the consciousness of enough of the cheering but unseeing 40 percenter base to save us all from 4 more years of the lying of this duplicitous Administration?

Or will Trump get to further pack the Supreme Court?

Or have the time to restrict more women's reproductive rights, including safe abortions?

Or time to ignore the urgent message from Mother Nature about the ongoing collapse of Earth's ability to serve the nearly 8 billion of us humans, 6 billion more than the 2 billion here when I was born in 1931?

Your call, Americans, but we can only pray you don't take the fear monger's lies as the way to the best future for our paycheck-to-paycheck fellow citizens and all the rest of us!

# CHAPTER 40 COVID-19 MAY SAVE OUR DEMOCRACY

*26 August 2020*

As the full impact of the Coronavirus became so evident, I wrote on July 6th that this pandemic could save our democracy. Let me repeat the crux of my arguments then:

> "I can't help thinking that for many of us the impact of Coronavirus did not really become apparent—certainly not to me and my family here in Washington DC—until sometime in March. Recently I found a restaurant receipt in my wallet dated March 6 which was the last time my wife and I had eaten at one of our favorite bistros. Egad! We felt so warmly toward many of those people in our favorite restaurants that we know they must be suffering keenly.
>
> It is that the significance of COVID-19 and the dreadful tv murder of George Floyd must be combined to offer all Americans the chance to save our weakened democracy from Trump's re-election on November 3rd!

What would have prevented a powerfully buoyant economy with a continuing great upturn in the US stock market from rendering Trump a landslide 2nd term?

Obviously, nothing including no shame at our unheeded racism!

And don't be surprised Trump partisans still give this dangerous, racist, populist that next 4 years which would allow for example him to further pack the US Supreme Court.

Let me make one major point which I as a white male who has been accorded countless unearned advantages.

That George Floyd's murder will hopefully rank as one of the major awakenings to whites here about the massive white failure to understand how people of color feel about the racism which whites—often unknowingly—practice daily!

Those of us (all of us??) must have watched the collapse of Trump in dealing with a real crisis such as Coronavirus. His failure to manage a coordinated national solution was scary, even to some of his 40% base.

> Who will defect and vote for a change, particularly, as his hatred and divide rhetoric keeps seeking support from his 40 percent base—many of whom are now badly impacted?
>
> It can only be hoped that the best instincts of all Americans can take succor from our best traditions and vote for a new President in November."

You can read my full July 6, 2020 piece here.

Since my July piece, many more of us have been affected and we have seen the repeated failed management of the Trump Administration in dealing with the virus with over 170,000 American deaths. These deaths represent 25% of all deaths from Covid in the world. The USA has only 4% of the world's population.

Perhaps, as you watch this week the continued claims of Trump's success at the Republican virtual convention, you will take a more accurate look at the character and motivations of the incumbent, who now owns the Republican Party!

Without that chance to see Trump's utter failure in facing this major pandemic challenge, it might have been that the prosperous economy he inherited from the Obama Biden years would have given him a free ticket to re-election.

In short, it has been this terrible virus which has exposed him and all his lifetime cronies and family who have been seen to treat our institutions as a chance to profit.

In the bright light of media coverage (no wonder he wants you to think the free press is "fake media") this terrible virus could be considered a gift of clarity beyond price.

The world's humans now number almost 8 billion, up from 2 billion at my birth in 1931 with many more people impacted more acutely than us around our overcrowded planet.

In case people think my earlier de-growth messages about our planet's incapacity to handle that number peacefully and democratically are no longer urgently in need of recognition and action, the current climactic events worldwide should disabuse them of that illusion. I hear nothing from the Trump side except their bloated claims of how great he has made things in his tenure.

Finally, if you happen to read my 8/23/20 piece, "We Need to Vote Biden in 2020" which is now currently on page one of this Church and State site, I strongly suggest you also listen to Amanpour and Company clip at the end of the Walter Isaacson interview of Kurt Andersen the author of Evil Geniuses, a book which explains so well how our present elites got so powerful and how the wealth gap got so dangerous.

# CHAPTER 41 WE NEED TO VOTE BIDEN IN 2020

*23 August 2020*

What percentage of Americans are now non-white? The answer is 40 percent and rising. Will race be the prime motivation for Trump's voters?

We will test that conjecture on November 3rd, but to me that should not be the major reason to select Biden.

The most descriptive analysis of motivation for bringing in Biden I have seen came to me from reading what was the August 23, 2020 page one NY Times book review of "Evil Enemies" by Kurt Andersen which postulates that political power has shifted, sadly often with many prominent Democratic polls concurrence, so far to the right elites that our democracy is failing and our unique abilities for innovation are now in danger of fading into failure!

You can read this review here. By the way, I have bought his book.

That Trump and the corporate powers he represents thus, perhaps unwittingly to many, become the visible surface boil on our nation's flesh—a startling lesion which desperately needs lancing!

Andersen's surprise at his own failure to see the elite power grab beginning decades ago gets a perhaps somewhat ambivalent echo from long time conservative George Will's Sunday 8/23/20 column in the Washington Post which describes our decline in power compared to China.

Will writes

> "A nation that nurtured elites that are at best ambivalent about their nation will not have sufficient confidence to inspire or deserve the confidence of other nations. Victor Nuland, former assistant secretary of state for European and Eurasian affairs, recalls George Kennan's 1946 'Long Telegram' in which he said that in opposing the then emerging Soviet threat 'much depends on the health and vigor of our own society'."

Nuland adds,

> "The first order of business is to restore the unity and confidence of US alliances in Europe and Asia."

Mr. Will concludes by writing:

> "Voters' principal consideration this year should be which presidential candidate is most apt to accomplish Nuland's

> recommendations. Although life is full of close calls this is not one of them".

Trump clearly fails everywhere by every comparison to our earlier leaders and now so unfavorably compared to his challenger Biden whose experience and expertise in foreign policy and in all matters of domestic governance is so overwhelmingly superior.

# ABOUT THE AUTHOR

Former U.S. Navy officer, banker and venture capitalist, Donald A. Collins, a freelance writer living in Washington, DC., has spent over 40 years working for women's reproductive health as a board member and/or officer of numerous family planning organizations including Planned Parenthood Federation of America, Guttmacher Institute, Family Health International and Ipas. Yale undergraduate, NYU MBA.

# ABOUT THE BOOK

This book is a compilation of the best articles out of many published on the Church and State website written about Donald Trump from late August 2020 the first time when author Collins recommended that readers vote for Joe Biden for President of the United States. Collins has a no holds barred perspective of close to four generations of progress in America. He has travelled the world extensively and seen the best and worst of humanity in many forms. He understands that the most likely scenario for failure of the American democratic system is for a dictator to emerge and seize power away from the people. He recommends, like many before him, that the United States should set an example by giving its people and all of the people in the world free contraceptives to empower women and reduce our human population painlessly from its nearly 8 billion today to 2 billion by 2100.

# FREE PREVIEW

Remember the famous Shakespeare play Macbeth in which the returning hero of war murders the king in order to become king and sets forth a series of events that lead him finally to understand what his humongous behavior has bought him when, at the suicide of his only truly close ally, his wife, he says: "Life's but a walking shadow, a poor player, / That struts and frets his hour upon the stage, / And then is heard no more. It is a tale / Told by an idiot, full of sound and fury, / Signifying nothing."

Donald J. Trump I imagine will likely never get there. He will never apologize. But in trying to murder our fragile democracy using hate, lying and his inherited wealth to take whatever route to power he could use, this disgraced former president is now faced as Macbeth was with an army of outraged citizens of both parties who are coming to displace him forever from political power and quite possibly put him in jail. Does he even have as Macbeth did any close ally?

Those elected officials who cluster about him in his coming precipitous fall must surely know their racist driven, power seeking fealty can't survive the morality test to which the majority of Americans will hold them!

Our democracy, despite the darkness of the political present, will survive and as we overcome the racism of 400 years of slavery, America will continue to show the world the vast benefits of our system of law and order even as we understand the heinous flaw of slavery which has always infected many world human populations since their inception!

We in time surprisingly may look back and thank Trump for exposing the worst in us so we could move on to fulfill the best in ourselves!

# KEYNOTE

By the time these Op Eds are read much will have changed. In fact, Trump may even be indicted for his behavior by some entity. But the arrogance that attended his Presidential term in office and his behavior afterward has had enormous effect on American politics which will malinger in our history forever. His role and influence in the January 6, 2021 U.S. Capitol insurrection will be marked in perpetual ignominy.

So why another book about facts which are now so well proven? Simply to state the urgency for repair, which to all who have read my op eds, to other possible audiences and raise the level of understanding which again perhaps is likely not to be present as time passes.

# OTHER BOOKS BY THE AUTHOR

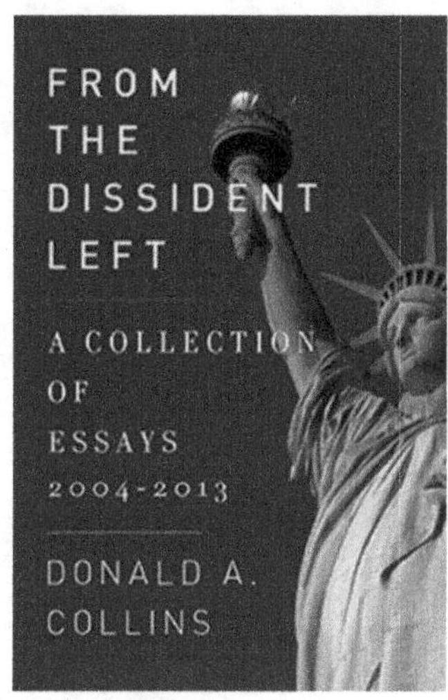


***From the Dissident Left: A Collection of Essays 2004-2013***

By Donald A. Collins
Publisher: Church and State Press (July 30, 2014)
ASIN: B00MA40TVE
Kindle Store